Creative Teaching
in the Lifelong Learning Sector

Creative Teaching Approaches in the Lifelong Learning Sector

Brendon Harvey and Josie Harvey

Mc Graw Hill Open University Press

Open University Press
McGraw-Hill Education
McGraw-Hill House
Shoppenhangers Road
Maidenhead
Berkshire
England
SL6 2QL

email: enquiries@openup.co.uk
world wide web: www.openup.co.uk

and Two Penn Plaza, New York, NY 10121-2289, USA

First published 2013

A catalogue record of this book is available from the British Library

ISBN-13: 9780335246304 (pb)
ISBN-10: 0335246303 (pb)
e-ISBN: 9780335246311

Library of Congress Cataloging-in-Publication Data
CIP data has been applied for

Typeset by Aptara Inc., India
Printed and bound by CPI Group (UK) Ltd, Croydon, CR0 4YY

Fictitious names of companies, products, people, characters and/or data that may be used herein (in case studies or in examples) are not intended to represent any real individual, company, product or event.

The *McGraw-Hill* Companies

For all the faces
in all our spaces
at all our places
public and private
this is for you

Praise for this book

"So much more than a manual or menu of how to bring creativity into teaching, this book will be refreshing for experienced lecturers, trainers and teachers, and an inspirational as well as reassuring font of ideas for those new to the role.

In addition to presenting practical ideas for individuals to use, Brendon Harvey and Josie Harvey's book is uniquely valuable in addressing institutional challenges that can face those introducing new creative ways of working, as well as providing counsel on how the lecturer/trainer/teacher can protect their own well-being when stepping into creative territory."

Dr Clare Rigg, Head of Department of Business, Hotel, Catering & Tourism, Institute of Technology Tralee, County Kerry, Ireland

"Brendon and Josie have drawn on their wealth of experience to co-author a practical teaching guide to meet the needs of 21st century learners in the Lifelong Learning Sector.

This is an excellent guide for both those new to teaching and also those seeking to meet the challenges of becoming more creative and using new technologies and social media more effectively in their professional practise. For the new teacher, there is a welcoming section addressing some of the anxieties which may be present before and during the early stages of practise as well as great examples of what to include in a creative session without breaking the bank!

The final section focuses on creativity within the organisational context and introduces us to the 'Trojan Mouse' and the benefits of action research.

This is a recommended read for anyone looking to update their practise."

Debbie Fletcher, Vice Principal of Leeds City College

"Drawing on their own experiences, as shared with us in the stories of their respective journeys from the world of traditional teaching and training methods and environments to that of creative active engagement of and with learners, the Harveys provide valuable insights into and a practical guide for learning facilitators in a variety of contexts to take or enhance their own journeys into the use of Creative Approaches in the Lifelong Learning Sector. Complete with stories, cases, and examples supported by provocative thinking points and activities and exercises for learning facilitators, this is a must-have resource. Consistent with their message, this is a creatively written and presented practical guide that inspires outside-the-box thought and action eschewing any attempts to provide "recipes" but rather championing the need for diversity of methods and approaches based on learners, setting, context, and other variables."

Tony G. LeTrent-Jones, Adjunct Professor, University of North
Carolina, USA, and Elon University, USA

Contents

About the authors

Brendon Harvey's involvement with education, research, and young people stretches back to his first teaching post in a Leeds school in 1980. Since then, he has taught in further education colleges, been a senior lecturer in three universities, and a post-doctoral researcher at the Centre for Inclusion and Diversity at the University of Bradford. In 1994, he started his own business, Aspects Associates, specializing in action learning and creativity for the public, private, and voluntary sectors. In 2005, he gained his PhD, a critical study of empowerment. Brendon's practice is split between consultancy/research, writing, and teaching. He is a Visiting Research Fellow at the Centre for Inclusion and Diversity at the University of Bradford, as well as an associate lecturer for Huddersfield University's School of Education and Professional Development in the UK and China.

Josie Harvey is a Senior Lecturer in the School of Education and Professional Development at the University of Huddersfield. She has taught on the full-time PGCE (Lifelong Learning) programme in the Post-Compulsory Education and Training (PCET) Department for the last five years, and has also been the TQEF leader for the Creativity and Innovation in Teaching in Higher Education project. She originally trained as an accountant before working in further and higher education, where she has acquired nearly 30 years of teaching experience across all levels and ages. She has also had 16 years' experience as a Senior Curriculum Manager in Business Studies in a large further education college, gaining extensive experience in staff development, curriculum design, and operations. She is also a co-author of the textbook *A Toolkit for Creative Teaching in Post Compulsory Education* (Eastwood et al., 2009).

Preface

The two of us were sat in a café in Leeds a couple of years ago, and over coffee started to recount some of the rich stories we had experienced in our collective sixty years of teaching. More and more, we realized we had a lot to offer new and existing teachers around creative teaching approaches and ways to engage students (as well as being able to identify the pitfalls) in many different sectors and organizations. We made a decision to capture this in a practical book for other teachers and trainers to use and adapt.

To set the backdrop to this book, we both felt it was valuable to share our own stories in teaching and creativity (or lack of it), so the reader can sense our passion and enthusiasm for these approaches in our teaching today.

Josie's story

My story begins with training as a chartered accountant back in the early 1980s. I remember many long days sitting in a lecture room being talked at and being crammed full of facts and exam techniques to pass the various professional papers in accountancy. At the time, I remembered what I needed to pass the exams by rote, but none of it made much sense – that came much later when I was actually preparing clients' accounts for real. I learnt my accountancy skills 'on the job', and might as well have skipped all those hours of frustration in a classroom for the amount of good it did me. After a few years in accountancy practice, I realized that it wasn't the profession for me and retrained as a teacher in the post-compulsory sector. I believed I could put my accounting knowledge to good use, giving my own students a very different classroom experience from my own. I certainly appreciated how difficult it was to make the subject accessible to all.

My teaching career in further education (FE) extended over twenty years. Before moving to the University of Huddersfield, I taught for sixteen years in a large FE college in the West Midlands whose catchment area was mainly from the inner city, and where over 50 per cent of the full-time students were from Black and Minority Ethnic (BME) communities. My students ranged in age from 16 to 60 years. I taught Accountancy and Business Studies on all types and levels of courses and qualifications. Classrooms were very diverse, and I often had challenging behaviour to deal with too. To engage, motivate, and encourage these learners to succeed, a wide range of teaching skills and approaches were required. For many years, I also had a senior management role, so teaching had to fit around other commitments, giving little time for extra preparation. Even so, student-centred learning and creativity in the classroom has always been key to my approach. I was fortunate to work alongside Geoff Petty, who was employed by the college for a while to bring his expertize and many of his teaching approaches from *Teaching Today* (1998). He had a major influence on my colleagues and me at that time. As a manager, I was responsible for the staff development of my team and the need for all of us to be 'outstanding' in the classroom when Ofsted arrived! Observing lessons made me realize how unimaginative some teaching could be, and the desperate need to move away from didactic, teacher-centred approaches to more fun, student-centred learning. All this played a large part in my research for my master's degree and later in my research into creativity in teaching at Huddersfield University.

In 2007, I moved from my FE college to Huddersfield University to begin leading a funded project entitled Creativity and Innovation in Teaching in Higher Education. The purpose of the project was to provide a basis for widening engagement with pedagogic innovation and to tap into a wider range of expertise and experience among staff across the University. This led to numerous 'Creativity Cafés' (see Chapter 9) where staff could network and share their creative teaching with others around different themes. One of the most significant developments to come out of the project was writing and collating the book *A Toolkit for Creative Teaching in Post Compulsory Education* (Eastwood et al., 2009) with five other colleagues. (The 'Learning Café' teaching approach is detailed in that book on page 21.) The book provided the basis for creative teaching approaches used with my own trainee teachers on the Pre-Service PGCE (Lifelong Learning) course at the University.

The research time on the project also gave me the opportunity to critically reflect (Schon, 1997) on my own teaching through the years, and explore existing literature on creative teaching. This solid grounding in research into creative teaching in post-compulsory education, coupled with my extensive experience in the classroom, has enabled me to develop creative approaches with both my own trainee teachers and my colleagues from within and outside the University, and has provided a rich source of material for this book.

Brendon's story

I was fortunate to be trained by leading exponents of student-centred learning in the 1970s. In my first post, an 11–18 comprehensive school in a city in the north of England, I was able to start using some of the skills of creativity and classroom management. It was a very different teaching environment from that of today in that there was no centralized curriculum, and a definite lack of performance management culture. When I moved to a further education college, I had developed a good grounding in involving students in their learning and in coping with the challenges of teaching a wide variety of adults and young people. Alongside my teaching of Communication Studies, I trained as a qualified counsellor to support my tutorial work. Here I was exposed to the work of American psychologist Carl Rogers, especially his classic work *Freedom to Learn* (1969), which stressed the importance of providing a creative space where individuals can flourish. After six years as a college lecturer, I moved on to my first university post in Management Development. As well as undergraduate and postgraduate courses, I became the lead tutor for a programme to train and accredit graduate management recruits for an international company. At this time, the early 1990s, both private and public sector companies were seeking competitive advantage through Total Quality Management (TQM) and other quality initiatives introduced by successful Japanese manufacturing companies. My research and practice embraced the softer skills of developing teams and so-called 'empowerment' of individuals. Due to the success of this work, I left the University and set up my own business. My 'students' were now drawn from all levels, not just senior and middle managers, but teams of shop floor workers and ancillary staff, from large companies to major government departments.

The thrust of this work was how to develop a culture of learning and involvement, sometimes in tough industrial environments. I began to sense a shift in my thinking. Senior managers were not always backing up how I was working with staff. The former talked about empowerment but did not cater for it in their actions or the work cultures they encouraged. My subsequent PhD research and published thesis studied three groups of managers who were experiencing such environments, and concluded on the types of learning spaces that needed to be created for individuals to grow and develop.

After returning to a full-time university post and working for the Open University as an Associate Lecturer, I revived my business but in a different direction. This time my work focus was driven much more by the needs of the public sector and I engaged in research and developing action learning for Criminal Justice and Drugs and Alcohol services. Small-group and individual interactions dominated. However, the main tenets of staying with the needs of individuals, developing creative approaches, and encouraging engagement still influenced my thinking and practice. My current work at the University of Huddersfield, within the School of Education and Professional Development, and at Bradford University as a Visiting Research Fellow at the Centre for Inclusion and Diversity, has continued to stimulate my quest to engage with a wide range of learners, in the UK and Asia, and ignite new creative approaches to learning and development for individuals and communities.

Acknowledgements

We would like to thank our colleagues in the School of Education and Professional Development and all our students who have studied on the Pre-Service PGCE/Cert.Ed. (Lifelong Learning) course at the University of Huddersfield. They have been instrumental and inspirational in helping us put this book together. Also a big thank you to the participants on the Creative Vocational Education project in China who have appreciated and challenged our creative teaching skills.

Introduction

The aim of this book is to offer creative teaching approaches to both trainee teachers and experienced tutors in the Lifelong Learning Sector (LLS). The authors are LLS practitioners who span different subject specialisms with a keen awareness and understanding of creativity in a rapidly evolving post-compulsory sector. We are conscious of the need for a text to support staff as they face the teaching and learning challenges within their practice environment. This is a practical book, drawing on the various techniques and environments to illustrate the many aspects of creative approaches for the Lifelong Learning Sector, rather than a series of case studies. Consequently, the book will appeal both to individual trainees and tutors working in this sector. The insights and conclusions drawn from the rich practice examples that are provided in the book will hopefully stimulate discussion on teacher training courses and staff development events focused on enhancing creative practice, classroom management, and learner engagement.

The Lifelong Learning Sector is broad in scope and diverse in both learner and setting. It includes further and higher education, work-based learning, adult and community settings, and encompasses vocational and academic subject areas both within and outside national curricula. Across all these settings it is acknowledged that teaching and learning has to embrace creativity to meet the variety of needs of its learners. Although the authors are based in the UK, they recognize that many of these issues, relating to greater use of creativity in LLS settings, also have an international focus. Other countries are also seeking new ways of creatively engaging diverse groups of learners and meeting the needs of different service sectors.

Some current publications offer a 'recipe' approach for new and experienced tutors, a catalogue of useful and often tried-and-tested creative activities that can be used within their practice setting. However, two things are missing from this marketplace provision: first, a shortage of texts that focus predominantly on the Lifelong Learning Sector, as opposed to the primary or secondary schools contexts; and second, a lack of publications that focus on the experiences of tutors and their learners as they engage in such creative activities. To extend the metaphor, the 'recipe' is provided but without any consideration of how the 'meal' is 'prepared, presented or digested'. Given the diversity of the Lifelong Learning Sector, it is important to identify the rationale of creative practices, the methods employed by practitioners, and what has worked in particular learning settings. Increasingly in the sector, in response to proposals to re-engage young adults in education, tutors are being required to focus on enhancing engagement with learners and tackle classroom management issues. For some, this has become a major challenge to existing practices. Exploring new ways of working, in addition to being aware of the potential pitfalls of creative practices in different settings, assist in meeting such challenges.

With the growth of new technology and its use in the classroom or training room, we have seen a plethora of new teaching platforms with the potential for learners to engage with staff, each other, and peers in other learning settings. Nevertheless, we have witnessed an over-reliance on the tried-and-tested, especially the use of PowerPoint. Learners potentially move from one PowerPoint presentation to another prepared by a different tutor. We are not adopting the position that all such methods are worthless learning tools. A good PowerPoint presentation can inspire learning and communicate knowledge. In addition, music and image can be incorporated to stimulate and enable learning experiences. It is the preponderance of this one way of directed learning that is at issue, with an 'active' tutor assuming that the 'passive' set of learners are still engaged by the time the twentieth slide is shown. Or that new knowledge has been comprehended and retained once the group of learners leaves the room clutching a handout of the presentation slides. We wish to encourage and breed confidence in tutors in LLS settings that there is another way. Such an approach is based upon a belief of what stimulates, excites, and engages learners. Moreover, we want to stress that tutors can get something out of it too, which is what makes teaching in such settings rewarding and fun. Preparing endless presentations based on a belief that the tutor knows best, or is the 'song-and-dance act', is energy sapping and mind numbing for all.

What is meant by creativity in teaching?

Asking such a question is rather like opening up Pandora's Box. The word 'creativity' is widely used today in many different ways. As Gibson (2005: 149) comments, creativity is 'a glimmer of hope and a word with which everyone can agree. Another hurrah word'. Craft et al. (2001: 39) identify four key environmental conditions for creative learning that have been

1. Challenge
2. Eliminate negative stress
3. High quality feedback
4. Live with uncertainty.

INTRODUCTION   **3**

helpful in shaping our own understanding of creative teaching and learning throughout this text. The first is the need to be challenged, by having goals set and being helped to set our own. Second, negative stress should be eliminated, as this prevents the brain functioning at a higher level. Third, there is a need for high-quality feedback to acquire self-knowledge, deepen our self-esteem, and continue to be motivated to learn. Finally, Craft and colleagues highlight the importance of having the capacity to live with uncertainty. Creative tutors cannot expect to have all the answers, but can offer robust and workable structures and processes to their learners. Therefore, in addition to fostering learner engagement, attention needs to be paid to the creative learning environment.

The outcomes from the two-year Teaching Quality Enhancement Fund (TQEF) research project led by Josie Harvey, exploring creativity and innovation in teaching in higher education, further assisted in shaping our understanding of creative teaching that moves beyond the creation of a learning environment. The TQEF research showed that creative teaching was multi-faceted with four broad categories. This understanding of creativity has proved to be beneficial when working with students and staff.

The Process of Creative Thinking	Creative Teaching Techniques	Creativity in Community and Employer Engagement	Creative and Innovative use of Technology in Teaching

Figure I.1 The four categories of creative teaching

Four broad categories of creative teaching can be identified (Figure I.1):

1   The process of creative thinking
2   Creative teaching techniques
3   Creativity in community and employer engagement
4   Creative and innovative use of technology in teaching.

First, we can regard creativity in teaching to be about making students think more creatively, to 'live outside the box', and to take risks with their ideas. Students are encouraged to analyse and sort problems out for themselves, to think laterally and find better ways of completing tasks. As Cropley (2001: 158) points out:

> people need to adjust to change that is both rapid and sweeping, both for their own well being and for that of societies in which they live ... to foster flexibility, openness, ability to cover novelty, ability to tolerate uncertainty and similar properties – in other words, creativity.

Second, creativity teaching can be interpreted as using innovative teaching techniques to engage the learners to learn, making it more fun and memorable. Cropley (2001: 160) notes that traditional education favours linguistic and logical-mathematical intelligence (left-brain learning), but neglects what Gardener (1993) calls 'intuitive' intelligence, which is a feature of the visual, imaginative, and holistic right-brain learning. We wish to redress this balance by using all the senses of our learners to nurture creativity.

Third, creative use is made of employer and community engagement to bring real-life case study scenarios into the curriculum, through problem-based and work-based learning. More and more, students need to possess problem-solving, independence, and critical thinking skills to deal with novel situations in organizations competing in 'highly competitive markets or in service industries that are underpinned by high levels of accountability' (Craft et al., 2001: 4).

Finally, it is important to emphasize the need to employ creative and innovative ways of bringing technology into the classroom, through utilizing potential learning platforms such as Facebook, Twitter, wikis, and the virtual learning environment, and thus facilitating communication between learners and tutors, their peers, and changing the way in which instructional resources might be organized and presented.

By adopting the above practices, it is possible to engage learners in their learning, introducing them to skills and experiences to equip them for a world requiring more transferable skills, enhanced by a creative-thinking mind.

An activity using these four catogories of creative teaching can be found in chapter 9, page 113.

Who will find this book useful?

If you are a *trainee teacher*, this book will be a valuable guide. We have not set out to write *the* textbook on creativity. Rather, we wish to offer a practical text that is rooted in our experience of which creative approaches work, and why. You will hopefully gain awareness from the sections that relate to confidence and the essentials of planning a creative session. We have been sensitive in establishing creative skills and tools that will enable you to develop your own distinctive style of working with learners.

If you are an *experienced tutor*, the book offers opportunities to reflect on your own ways of working with learners. The authors are conscious of the demands being placed on LLS tutors at this time. We hope that experienced tutors are able to add to their repertoire of skills through using this book; it contributes to continuing professional development objectives, and stimulates fresh ideas to engage your learners, both now and in the future.

If you are a *teacher trainer*, the book offers something more than traditional texts on teaching and learning. Through its considerations of the organizational context, trainees can be encouraged to explore the significance of the creative environment in different LLS organizational settings, as well as the importance of their professional wellbeing. Throughout each chapter there are reflective prompts to encourage you to look at your emerging practice and engage with creative approaches.

How the book is organized

The book is divided into three parts:

- Part 1: The Individual
- Part 2: The Group Perspective
- Part 3: The Organizational Context.

These three aspects of practice have been deliberately separated so that they can be explored in depth, although we recognize the interrelationships between them. The reader is helped to see these links through the frequent use of symbols and cross-referencing notes in the text.

Part 1: The Individual

Chapter 1, 'Creative Learning Spaces', highlights the importance of seeing creativity not as something that is *done to* learners but more an approach to craft a particular type of creative space where learning can flourish.

Chapter 2, 'Reflecting on You in the Creative Learning Setting', turns the spotlight on tutors. They are encouraged and guided to reflect on how they communicate with learners, identify their competences, and avoid the misconception of the creative tutor as a 'song-and-dance act'. The chapter identifies the characteristics of a creative tutor.

Chapter 3, 'Confidence and Creativity', addresses characteristics of confidence and offers practical guidance on how it can be boosted. In particular, the links between confidence and fostering creativity in learning settings are explored.

Part 2: The Group Perspective

Chapter 4, 'Introduction to Groups', is the essential primer for this part of the book. Here the social pedagogic approach to working with learners is discussed in the context of the Lifelong Learning Sector. The value of learning in groups is emphasized, especially in relation to developing employability and meeting the needs of diverse learners.

Chapter 5, 'Classroom Management and Creativity', sets out the fundamental characteristics of a productive creative learning space, and how potential problems of classroom management can be solved by learner engagement and consideration of the physical space.

Chapter 6, 'The Hooks of Engagement', offers different creative methods to ignite the spark of creativity in learners and get them engaged in learning. This chapter reaffirms a strong theme of the book – the creative tutor finding out from groups what excites, what engages interest, what makes learning fun and enjoyable.

Chapter 7, 'Encouraging Constructive Thinking and Exploration of Ideas', firmly places the emphasis on the learner as an active inquirer, not a passive sponge! Various creative approaches are described to stimulate constructive thinking, engage with difference, and puzzle and question. The benefits and drawbacks of each approach are examined, based on the authors' experience within LLS settings.

Chapter 8, 'Creative Beginnings and Endings', focuses on different approaches to starting and ending a creative session. In particular, the ways in which the creative tutor enables the session to flow, helps build group identity, and promotes learner awareness of the need for recognition of learning within a group setting.

Chapter 9, 'Designing a Creative Session', aims to support the creative tutor in the task of constructing a session that embraces the needs of diverse LLS learners. The potential methods, resources, and assessment requirements of creative approaches are discussed. In addition, the design considerations of using creative approaches with large groups are highlighted.

Part 3: The Organizational Context

Chapter 10, 'Stimulating Creative Change in Your Practice', turns the reader's attention towards the organizational context, especially in relation to introducing creative approaches, and what helps and hinders innovation in LLS settings. The tutor is encouraged to reach out to other creative practitioners to capture and share learning. An action-learning framework is offered to focus energy and encourage collaboration.

Finally, Chapter 11, 'Looking after the Creative Tutor', is designed to promote a sense of cautious optimism. Creative tutors are special; they open up different possibilities for diverse groups of learners, and often give a lot of themselves in the process. Consequently, the creative tutor needs resilience. The chapter offers advice on self-care strategies to prevent professional burnout and promote tutor wellbeing.

An explanation of the symbols used throughout the book

 The cloud symbol is used where the reader is encouraged to take part in an activity or reflect on an aspect of their teaching relating to the topic being discussed.

 Occasionally, the scroll symbol has been used in the book. This indicates where extra activities are available around the topic being discussed. These activities are located at the end of that chapter.

 This symbol is used extensively throughout the book to link together related topics in different chapters. The page number is quoted to make this search easier for the reader.

 This symbol has been used to identify sections in the book that refer to developing employability skills in the learner.

Use of terminology

We believe it is important to justify the use of certain terms used in the book. These include:

- *Learner*: The term 'learner' rather than 'student' is used throughout the book because in LLS settings a variety of different titles can be given to participants, including students, trainees, delegates, and pupils. Therefore, to increase clarity we use the term 'learner' to encompass all these labels, as they all take part in the learning process.
- *Tutor*: The term 'tutor' rather than 'teacher' is used throughout the book because different labels are used in the wide range of LLS settings, including teachers, lecturers, trainers, and consultants. Thus we use the unified term 'tutor' to make it less confusing for the reader.
- *Learning space*: The term 'learning space' rather than 'classroom' is used throughout the book because in LLS settings a range of places can be used for teaching, such as classrooms, IT learning

centres, community halls, and conference rooms. The term 'learning space' encompasses them all.

- *Session*: The term 'session' rather than 'lesson' is used throughout the book because quite often in the LLS the context may be outside the traditional setting of a college, school or university. Instead, the setting may be a conference, a training agency or a community centre, and therefore the term 'session' is more appropriate.

Part 1

The Individual

1 Creative Learning Spaces

Imagine an actor walking onto a stage. The theatre is closed and the production she is a part of is about to start rehearsals. She is alone there in that space for that moment. The part has been written. The actor knows what she should be saying because she is clutching a script that details all the words and stage directions. Looking around, the actor may consider who else she is working with, what the demands of the director are, how this space makes her feel, what the audiences are going to be like, how confident she feels. Ultimately, what is going to be created in this space by this group interacting with each other, guided by a script, with expectations of a director and an audience? Now, consider an individual tutor walking into a learning space. A curriculum, or scheme of work, may already have been decided upon. He looks around at the space where he will interact with others, who include the learners (himself included) and an 'audience' of various stakeholders, for example, an employer or parent, eager to see a successful production. He is both actor and director, following at times a very rigid script that is not to be deviated from, or he may have more scope to develop and direct a different sort of production. In most cases, this 'stage' – the learning space – has the potential for a range of experiences. This chapter considers what constitutes this space. In particular, what can make this a *creative* space?

Physicist David Bohm (1998) links creativity closely to perception and the recognition of new phenomena. To achieve this, Bohm argues, a state of mind needs to exist that is 'attentive, alert, aware and sensitive'. We discuss awareness for the creative practitioner later in Part 1, suffice it to say that merely being aware is not enough to spur on change. Learners may be aware of where they need to develop but critically they may not know how to conduct that change. To do this they may have to challenge previous beliefs or behaviours – and embrace new ones. At the same time they have to foster existing skills – communicating with others, writing and compositional skills, time management – to make fresh decisions and achieve new goals in their academic writing, presenting skills or in the engineering workshop.

Three perspectives on creative learning spaces

Through this discussion we can see that creativity is linked to *a mental space*, a place where suspending judgement, allowing new possibilities to emerge, and becoming clear and being open to new learning are manifest. Unfortunately, old scripts emerge to constrict this space: self-talk of 'I can't do this', 'I'm not good enough', 'people of my age/class/gender don't . . .'; or others' perceptions (tutor, parent, partner, peers) impose their own meanings onto that space. Again, both the learner and the tutor are subject to the possibility of negative self-talk and the pressure of others.

Physical space is also important if creativity is to influence individual learning. A teaching or training room that is constricted by its floor area, large immovable furniture, and limited wall space presents a challenge. This is not insurmountable, however. A colleague of ours when once faced with tables bolted to the floor brought a socket set into the room and got the group to unfasten the tables and create a space for the activities they were engaging in! At the end of the two-hour session the room was quickly put back together (although this is not so appealing when the session lasts just for forty minutes!). This story illustrates a key point: that as a creative tutor it is important to consider the physical space carefully and determine how it could be utilized effectively. For example, is the furniture arranged to enable interaction between learners? Overall, the question to be asked is, does this space enable the planned creative activity?

Thinking points

If you have fixed desks, can you rearrange the chairs to create a new physical space? For example, turn them around or move them out to the front of the class in a circle or cluster.

The *space between* is a third form of space and it is where the learner–tutor and learner–peer relationships function. As we have touched upon above, creativity requires consideration of a mental space. Both partners in learning have these mental spaces but it is where they interact that is the 'space between'. Within this space the tutor operates to guide, inform, provide feedback, and encourage. The learner may also enter this space to question, inform, provide feedback, and encourage others. For us, this idea of a 'space between' is crucial in determining the relationship between tutor and learner and between learner and peers. Throughout the book we will return to this guiding concept. It helps us to ensure that creativity is relational, that it often emerges out of a joint working between learner and learner or tutor and learner.

Too many inexperienced tutors (and some experienced ones, too) see that as a one-way relationship, with responsibility for learning on the shoulders of the tutor. It is they who prepare materials, take responsibility for ground rules, lead their group, provide feedback on performance, and assess outcomes. If we consider the 'space between', however, this role changes. Materials do not always have to be prepared by the tutor. Often the activity can intrinsically involve the learner – they can set up, make materials as part of the task, and keep time. Ground rules can be jointly constructed and owned. (Ground rules are discussed in Chapter 5, 'Classroom Management and Creativity', p. 46.)

Individually or collectively leading a session can be shared, or solely be the responsibility of the learners. They can step into the space and take the lead. Developing learners' feedback skills is important, as it helps them to recognize the criteria of success and to practise vital communication skills, thus contributing to a supportive learning environment. Such practice also sends a powerful message to learners: that learning is not the sole responsibility of the tutor. Learners need to take responsibility for their own development and that of their peers. Furthermore, the impact of peer support and challenge (where it is sensitively administered) can be far-reaching. For some, it may outweigh what the tutor has to say.

Therefore, such a creative learning space is dynamic, negotiated, potentially exciting, and, we would argue, offers tremendous potential for learning that has real impact. When working one-to-one, in small or large groups, or through virtual learning platforms, this 'space between' exists. Careful nurturing and management of the space is important to ensure it retains its qualities and potential. Re-addressing ground rules, and the tutor being critically reflective of facilitation skills, are tools to ensure the space is honoured.

2   Reflecting on You in the Creative Learning Setting

Use of non-verbal communication and body language

Here, we discuss a recent example of working with a group of tutors to emphasize the importance of reflecting on the creative learning setting.

The group was asked to consider how their non-verbal communication influenced the responses of the learners they taught. One participant volunteered to sit on a chair and role-play the learner, while another participant agreed to be the 'tutor'. The other members of the group, the observers, were then tasked to watch the 'tutor' and note a particular aspect of non-verbal communication – the tone of voice, facial expression, gesture, posture, use of space.

The 'tutor' was asked to role-play a situation in which he fed back to the learner an unsatisfactory piece of coursework the tutor had just assessed. To make the learning more evident, however, the tutor was asked to over-exaggerate so as to completely demotivate the learner, making her unable to positively address a revision of the work submitted. It was quite disturbing how quickly the 'tutor' got into role. Lots of data were generated, the observers noting ways in which a sarcastic comment or foreboding presence could influence the subsequent behaviour of the learner. By ex-aggerating the situation, it was then easier to identify an alternative, more effective way of dealing with the learner. Such communication would engender a more positive learner response, encouraging her to learn from the piece of coursework submitted.

The same exercise was repeated, but with the observers coaching the 'tutor' to focus on his non-verbal communication (NVC) so as to be more supportive of the learner, without losing the importance of providing critical feedback. This time, the tutor's voice was quieter and far more developmental in tone. Rather than standing over the learner pointing to an area of revision without referring to the piece of work submitted, he sat down slightly to the side of the learner with the assessment in front of them. The group concluded that the activity had increased their awareness of how their body language may influence learners' responses and subsequent development.

You may think that having such self-awareness is basic good teaching practice. Although this is true, a creative learning setting requires an even greater sense of self-awareness, and the following section explains why this is so.

Thinking points

Pick one of your learning settings. How might your body language influence how you interact? Could you find out? Which methods might you use?

Characteristics of a creative tutor

Let us consider again our understanding of creativity. We are seeking to do things differently, to spring a surprise, to initiate change. We are hoping our learners are going to embrace a new way of learning, to take more responsibility for that learning, and to engage with themselves and others in learning situations that they may never have encountered before. That requires a leap of faith on their part. When they enter the creative spaces we are initially providing, we are greeting them with difference and uncertainty.

Different in that it may be like no other learning space they have come across before, one where they are being invited to be different – active learners rather than passive recipients. The space may also therefore be full of uncertainty. How will the learners behave? Will there be a lack of control? If a tutor comes into the classroom day after day with the same session format, which is then repeated when the learners move on to the next class of the day, it is unsurprising that this form of learning becomes the norm. It is what the learner expects. As a creative practitioner, you should instead present an alternative experience that will help the learner out of this pattern. As a trainee teacher, you may also share the same perceptions of learning. Who are the role models for you? Of course, this will depend on what you have experienced as a learner, whether as an

Figure 2.1 Characteristics of a creative teacher

engineer being trained on the job or a law student fresh from a degree programme. De Bono comments:

> In school we are always asking students to judge, to categorize, to analyze and dissect. There is far less emphasis on exploration, possibility, generation, creativity and design. There is more emphasis on what things are than on what you can make things be.
>
> (De Bono 1995: 94-5)

So how can we engender the trust of learners in their peers and ourselves? We may need to ensure that even though doubts are harboured (we do not give up such learning habits easily), this learning experience is going to be worth engaging in.

Fautley and Savage (2007) usefully identify nine characteristics of a creative teacher (see Figure 2.1). In the light of this, it is important to question how we might view some of these qualities through the 'lens' of the Lifelong Learning Sector.

Regarding being *inspirational*, Fautley and Savage describe the need for 'presenting knowledge', but in the Lifelong Learning Sector this is to be extended to engaging with learners in a way that seeks to redress some of the learning experiences, or re-ignite others, they have experienced. The LLS student body is diverse, including, for example, adults re-entering training and development after a break from formal learning, or, alternatively, young people who have decided to attend a college instead of continuing with school post 16 years of age. Some learners may not have chosen to attend; they may have had to attend as part of a government- or business-sponsored programme. Tutors may come face to face with two sets of learners, say young and older adults, in the same group. Therefore, learning needs to be presented as fun and worthwhile. The other related characteristics of *being an encourager* and *stimulating curiosity* are part of this creative package that tutors present their learners with.

Since in the Lifelong Learning Sector we often need to *raise learners' expectations* (either because of previous experiences of learning at school or training, or because they are from disadvantaged backgrounds), the creative tutor has the ideal opportunity to present different learning scenarios and allow learners to engage with their peers and tutor using novel methods. In her book *Estates* (2008), Lynsey Hanley describes the barriers to the advancement of a young working-class pupil at her sixth-form college. Her tutors recognized something in her, a curiosity, a sense she could develop if she put her mind to it. The struggle for her was to demolish the 'wall in her head', the belief that people like her, from the housing estate she came from, did not go beyond the physical and mental wall of the estate.

In conclusion, although the characteristics in Figure 2.1 were originally applied to secondary education, all of these would hold for a creative practitioner in the Lifelong Learning Sector with a particular emphasis being placed on the inspiring, encouraging tutor stimulating curiosity in his or her learners. In addition, we feel it is important to add the skills and qualities of the process expert.

In the example of the non-verbal communication activity that opened this chapter, the learners were tasked with various roles around the exploration of a concept. The tutor role was both subject 'expert' and facilitator of the process. It is the skilful execution of the latter that enables learners to feel secure and guided. The learners were briefed clearly on what they were expected to do and the activity was facilitated within a timed and structured session.

Such a framework forms the boundary of the creative space. The facilitator is aware of what such boundaries consist of and guides individual learners, especially those new to such learning activity, within that framework. Although a degree of 'handholding' is inevitable, until trust and learner confidence grow (especially with new groups), the use of ground rules is a further characteristic of a creative tutor. Ground rules are the agreed guidelines of behaviour and commitment between tutor and learners (such as listening and respecting others), and these are covered in greater depth in Chapter 5, 'Classroom Management and Creativity' (p. 46), where we explore the role of creativity in working with groups. For present purposes, however, it is important to emphasize that the tutor offers the opportunity for ground rules to be developed – ideally with the learners contributing to them. Most learners have a keen sense of what they regard as helpful and unhelpful behaviours in a learning setting. Try to tap into this sense of how they wish things to be, and then prompt them if they miss out those that are important for you as their tutor. Ground rules become the process rules of practice, clearly aiding understanding of the expectations of both tutor and learners within that setting.

There is a myth that creativity (and by implication the 'creative') is woolly and undisciplined in practice. However, many artists – whether they be dancers, authors, painters, actors or musicians – are extremely disciplined in how they work. The surety of the process – not the activity that takes place within it, or uncertainty of outcomes that may result – is a hallmark of creative practice. And for a tutor it is no different: working with activities and dealing with emergent situations with skill and sensitivity enables learners to feel secure. Such practice is a lifelong pursuit, as the unpredictability of working creatively throws up new challenges when working with individuals and groups.

Being conscious of your competence

We have stressed the importance of the tutor being aware of how he or she develops trust in a creative space. In addition, the need for process skills in designing and leading student-centred creative activities demands a heightened sense of awareness from the tutor in relation to the individual and group dynamics of learners. If a tutor walks into a classroom with a PowerPoint presentation and runs through endless slides, engaging infrequently with students, then departs without consideration of whether any learning has taken place, self-awareness will not have featured. Thankfully, creative learning spaces are potentially more enriching, for both learners and tutors – both are learners, and this point cannot be stressed enough. If the tutor adopts this attitude towards their practice, they are likely to be more 'present' in acting and reacting to emerging situations in the learning setting. Such creative situations could be characterized by obvious engagement and learning, or potentially the opposite – learners confused and an increased risk of disengagement. In both cases, tutors need to be conscious of their competence.

Figure 2.2 demonstrates four levels of awareness and how these relate to competence. The grid represents four different positions relating to the awareness of the tutor and their degree of competence:

Position 1. The tutor is unaware that they are struggling with their teaching. They may be thinking that a good job is being done and that learning is taking place, a head-in-the-sand attitude. The possible learner dissatisfaction can be explained by the latter not wanting to engage, or the pigeonholing of particular groups by the tutor. For example, a tutor may have fixed views about certain groups of learners, characterized by the

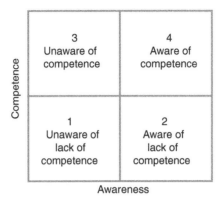

Figure 2.2 Four levels of awareness on the part of the tutor

subject grouping ('typical of engineers'), age ('you can't do game-like activities with adults') or gender ('they are all lads in that group'). Little feedback or support may be on offer for this tutor, so development of their skills is hampered.

Position 2. The tutor knows that they are struggling with their teaching. The learners may not be engaging with their methods and they see the results: poor attendance and timekeeping, half-hearted involvement in activities, lack of learning and development of the learners. It could be that the tutor has been too ambitious, has not prepared thoroughly, or lacks the process skills to deal with emergent outcomes in a creative setting. For example, the creative activity, say a role-play or game, opens up a discussion that the tutor had not planned for. So their response is to shut that potential learning down and stick to the plan, instead of thinking on their feet and seeing how generative this avenue of learning could be. In order to develop, this tutor has achieved their first goal, the awareness of the need to change. The second goal is to find out how they can change, what development opportunities are available (formal and informal), and then gain support for the change.

Position 3. The tutor may have taught this way for a great deal of their career. It is part of who they are and, if asked, they might not be able to pin down what works (or maybe it does not concern them), but they see the results. Learners enjoy their sessions, are learning and developing through the approach being adopted. This may seem a good position to be in, which it is to some extent. The opportunity for this tutor to help the tutor who is experiencing Position 1 or 2 above is limited, however. They do not really view themselves working with the learners (or with other staff); they may be focused totally on their own outcomes. The lack of sharing of experience and skill prohibits joint learning and development of a core team of creative tutors. Such isolation may serve the individual tutor and the learner while they are in their classes, but the provision of education and development becomes a lottery – dependent on whom the learners have as a tutor.

Position 4. Having a keen sense of the tutor as an evolving practitioner has real benefits. There is the potential for the tutor to be paired with other, less competent colleagues so they can support their development. Ideas and practices can be shared across teams and settings. Being competent and aware allows recognition of the fact that although learning and development are taking place in learners, enabled by creative practice, the tutor is not the finished article. Learning settings change, and the learner body evolves. For instance, witness the effects on many colleges that now teach to the 14–19 agenda, or the increasing rates of young people who cannot gain employment even though they have fulfilled the first hurdle of gaining qualifications and experience. Therefore, increasing competence is needed by the tutor to engage and motivate a diverse range of learners. Such structural changes impact on learning settings and learner behaviour. Increasingly, the tutor needs to employ a variety of approaches to serve the needs of these learners. Moreover, these need to be prevented from going into management! Often this is the only career path for the competent tutor. This normally means less time in the classroom and at the interface with learners, and, instead, a transfer to the static tedium of the management meeting room. If good creative practice is to be developed and burnout avoided, such tutors need to be carefully managed both by self and others, not be given even more work, while less competent tutors escape with lighter workloads. This is explored further in Chapter 11, 'Looking after the Creative Tutor' (p. 137).

Avoid the song-and-dance act

The following narrative relates to a training programme we ran for in-service tutors in the vocational education sector. The programme consisted of introducing them to creative ways of teaching and fostering a more student-centred approach to their practice. The training was to culminate in a 'mini-lesson', in which a team of four trainees would creatively involve the other members of the group, playing the role of their learners, in a creative learning experience. Most of the teams got the 'learners' involved throughout with some 'tutor input' but mainly the sessions were

The Song and Dance Act

activity-packed and skilfully facilitated. The last team got ready for their 'mini-lesson'. It opened with a trainee embarking on a frenzied act of enthusiastic performance, which was designed to startle and arouse curiosity in the 'learners'. Other team members looked on. It was impressive for the first five minutes. However, thirty-five minutes later the 'learners' were beginning to tire of the wave of energy. The trainee was also feeling the pace, as he began to perspire and his voice began to crack. A hurried learner activity was frequently interrupted by another intervention by the trainee, and therefore did not enable a great deal of learning to take place. What was going on here?

Put simply, the trainee was trying to do too much. He had interpreted the concept of creativity as believing it was up to him to impart all his energy into the learner. He had to be an act: a 'song-and-dance' merchant who would startle (he did that!) and cajole the learner into engaging through his performance alone. We are not saying that if a tutor has a talent, whether for music or performance, he or she should feel prevented from exhibiting it. Many tutors are drawn to creative practice because they feel that such skills are not being used in a classroom setting. Or some are complete extroverts, full stop!

It is a matter of balance between your use of the creative space and how learners occupy and contribute to that space:

- If it is *all you*, the learners (either individually or in groups) will not have the opportunity to explore for themselves what is being presented, or probe questions or ideas they may have of their own.
- Moreover, the well-intentioned entertainer is not considering learning. Energy is expended on the input, rather than enabling and assessing, prompting and encouraging.

Thinking points

A key reflective question for the tutor to ask themselves, at any point in a learning session, is: 'Just who is doing all the work here?'

If a tutor realizes that they have been dominating the session for too long, a change of pace is needed as well as the involvement of the learners. There is a further consideration here. Part of the feedback given to the trainee teacher, in the example described above, was for him to consider whether he could keep up such a performance, session after session, without having a detrimental effect on himself. The learning from Position 4 identified above – the competent aware tutor – focused on the need for wellbeing. Being the 'song-and-dance act' can potentially be entertaining. But, it may also prevent learners and tutors sustaining healthy learning habits that ensure really effective performance. We address this, and the activities that could prevent it from happening, in Chapter 9, 'Designing a Creative Session' (p. 88).

3   Confidence and Creativity

To be creative and to take risks with new approaches and activities, tutors need to feel confident with their learners. Also, for student-centred creative activities to be successful, learners have to feel supported and confident too. If the behaviour of the tutor is threatening or unsupportive, learners may be reluctant to respond and will become demotivated. For learners to participate in creative and interactive tasks, they will not want to fear being ridiculed, or risk having their self-esteem lowered, especially in front of their peers. Therefore, a comfortable and trusting environment is vital.

This chapter focuses on the confidence of tutors. We consider some of the issues that can lower their confidence, as well as boost it. Awareness of their own confidence can play a major part in tutors' attitude and approach towards their own learners in the classroom, and we address how this awareness can be used to improve learners' self-esteem and motivation. The lack of confidence of many tutors, especially at the start of their teaching qualification, is outlined in the example below.

On one course we teach, every year at Induction, a group of trainee teachers completes a 'Hopes and Fears' exercise whereby they write a letter to themselves. In this letter they have to voice their 'hopes and fears' for the course ahead. The letter is sealed in an envelope until the last day of the course, when it is reopened to assist them in revisiting their teaching experiences and 'learning journey'.

Before the envelope is sealed on that first day, each trainee teacher writes five key words or phrases from their letter onto individual sticky notes and attaches the notes to the classroom wall, clustering them into similar themes. The biggest cluster always relates to 'lack of confidence', 'anxiety', and 'ability to teach'. When they revisit their letters at the end of the course, the group members often reflect on the unnecessary fears they had about their confidence. The issues that did affect them on their placements, such as time management and working with other staff, were never mentioned. At least most walked away from the course much more confident and creative in their teaching, even if other issues remained.

Developing confidence in the classroom

This chapter explores the relationship between confidence and being creative. Tutors need confidence to be creative. Tutors and learners do not easily move out of their comfort zone, but if both are to be creative both need to feel confident.

What do we mean by confidence? What are some of the issues facing the tutor, including self-concept and self-awareness in relation to effective teaching?

The activities in this chapter will help highlight issues of self-confidence and will encourage awareness of the positive attributes and strengths that tutors have to offer. A positive approach to self-image will help confidence to grow and, subsequently, will encourage more risk-taking within creative teaching activities. If tutors are aware of their own confidence issues, it will help them to be aware of their learners' self-esteem issues too. The activities will provide a practical guide to help develop and boost levels of confidence in both tutors and their learners, and therefore provide the courage to use more creative teaching approaches in the classroom.

Confidence and some of the issues surrounding it

The word 'confidence' (or rather, lack of it) resonates very loudly, especially with trainee teachers and newly qualified teachers, as highlighted in the example at the beginning of this chapter. Issues of confidence can also affect more experienced tutors who are faced with changes to teaching practices through curriculum redesign or shifts in the learner demographic. For example, a tutor could be wedded to their didactic style (i.e. the tutor's viewpoint prevails) but is now required to embrace a curriculum that is based on a more student-centred pedagogy. Or a tutor used to teaching adults finds herself faced by a group of 14-year-old learners.

What do we mean by 'confidence'? The *Concise Oxford English Dictionary* (2008) defines confidence as 'a positive feeling arising from an appreciation of one's own abilities; self-assurance'. Another definition is 'calmness and assertiveness during social interaction' (Manning and Ray, 1993: 180). Although these two definitions focus slightly differently on the meaning of confidence, they both share that element of surety in oneself.

What are confident people like? What are their qualities and how do they behave?

Thinking points

Divide your learners into three groups and ask them to think of a confident person they know. With that person in mind, ask each group to consider one of the questions below:

1   What are confident people like?
2   What qualities do they have?
3   How do they behave?

Some responses to these questions by a group studying for a teaching qualification in Lifelong Learning are presented below. The responses provide an insight into the trainee teachers' perceptions of confidence.

When asked what confident people are like, they replied:

- Have a presence
- Leaders
- Successful
- Convincing
- Ambitious
- Comfortable in their own skin
- Charismatic
- Secure
- Opinionated

Not all of the responses were necessarily positive, but all reflected strong characteristics. There is a danger that over-confident traits such as 'opinionated' and 'ambitious' can have a negative impact on people, and can be off-putting to others. So empathy with and awareness of the learner group are important characteristics to develop if you want the learners to respond positively to you.

When asked what qualities a confident person has, the trainee teachers' responses included:

- Relaxed
- Friendly
- Positive body language
- Good listeners
- Leadership management
- Arrogant
- Likeable
- Humorous
- Spontaneous
- Approachable

The positive qualities the trainee teachers recognized in confident people included open body language with good eye contact, a relaxed and friendly stance. However, not all responses would be regarded as beneficial qualities, such as 'arrogance'. Again, it can be a fine line between qualities that are desired and valued by others and those that are not. If tutors are likeable, approachable, supportive, and good listeners, learners are more likely to respond positively and welcome teaching sessions that are more creative and student-centred.

When asked what behaviours confident people display, the trainee teachers responded:

- Effortless
- Easy-going
- Walk tall
- In control
- Natural in social situations
- Overpowering
- Openness
- Warmth

Many of these responses indicate the behaviour needed to develop confidence, although not to be 'overpowering'. Developing confidence will raise self-esteem where it is low, but an awareness of being over-confident is also important. Furthermore, an imbalance between the confidence of the tutor and learner can cause apprehension and reticence on the part of both.

Once confidence grows in a tutor, experimenting with creative teaching approaches is more likely.

> Attempt the Confidence Quiz on p. 35 to plot your confidence level in the different areas. Add other categories, if they are appropriate, such as 'confidence as a parent'.
>
> This exercise helps to identify areas that need to be developed to help raise one's overall confidence.

Few people are totally confident in all areas of their lives at all times. As Grunfield (2006: 160) says:

> None of us feel confident in all fields ... In the areas in which you don't feel confident you tend to avoid taking risks because you don't expect to be successful. You rely on the approval of others to feel good about yourself and yet at the same time you discount or ignore compliments that are paid to you.

This is what can happen in learning spaces. If there is a lack of confidence, there can be a tendency to follow the same tried-and-tested 'safe' option, rather than experimenting with new creative approaches. Often, the main focus of the learner is on the negative thoughts and outcomes, however small, and any positive occurrences or praise given, however large, tend to be forgotten.

Reasons for lack of confidence

Research by Norman and Hyland (2003: 267) with Initial Teacher Training (ITT) learners identified the following characteristics regarding their lack of confidence:

- Self-critical and doubtful of their own abilities
- Anxious, nervous, tense, uncomfortable, and insecure
- Difficulty communicating with and interacting with others
- Avoidance of certain tasks.

The responses of our trainee teachers in the Lifelong Learning Sector about lacking confidence in teaching echo some of the themes identified by Norman and Hyland (2003):

- The newness of task and the strangeness of teaching. Many were only just starting their placements. They were anxious about their learner groups and the ability to stand up and teach them. Worried that they would look nervous, be tongue-tied, and not cope with the class.
- Not feeling like a tutor. Some were concerned about fitting in with the existing staff, and also being accepted by the learners. Many worried that learners would resent a new trainee teacher and would have preferred to keep their experienced one. Some felt they looked too young to command authority over LLS learners, while others were concerned about other aspects of their appearance.
- Many expected too much from themselves and their learners, and over-estimated the amount of preparation they needed to do. They were also anxious about their ability and level of knowledge.
- Being judged constantly by tutors, mentors, peers, and learners was another concern. They were nervous about the lesson observations, and feedback from mentors and peers.
- Uncertainty of being successful. They had concerns about completing the course successfully and being liked and supported by their peers.
- Anxiety around using new technology. The growth of social networking sites and virtual learning environments can be daunting for the older tutor.
- Negative self-talk. Previous bad experiences can cause confidence to be dented. Some had had negative attitudes embedded into their mindset from their families, social background or peers.

Although these themes were the responses of trainee tutors, many newly qualified tutors would recognize some of these anxieties, as would even more experienced tutors. Addressing some of these concerns is the first step to confidence.

How to boost confidence

So what is the way forward? The answer lies in focusing on the positives, and linking with people who will support you.

Try the exercise below to identify what the 'confident you' would look like.

Thinking points

When you have built up your confidence, what will you be like? What qualities will you have and how will you behave?

What will you be doing that you aren't at the moment, or how will you be doing it better?

By whatever means you prefer (e.g. draw a picture), represent your 'confident self' on a sheet of paper. The more colourful and imaginative the better!

List three benefits of being more confident.

Now you have identified the 'confident you', how are you going to achieve it? The next exercise will help you to focus on your positives.

Thinking points

List 10 positive statements about yourself.

If you are stuck, here are some words to help you get started!

Generous, hard-working, supportive, honest, friendly, good-tempered, fun . . .

Now it is time to identify your skills and achievements to date.

Thinking points

List your skills and achievements under the following headings:

- Education and Training
- Hobbies and Interests
- Work
- Involvement in the Community
- The Family

These two exercises help address self-image, focusing on the good qualities a person has. Using them to good effect to help boost confidence is the key.

To develop confidence, focus on the positive qualities and skills, but recognize and then address any negative self-talk. Automatic Negative Thoughts (ANTs) is a term used in cognitive behaviour therapy, and often linked to research on depression, fatigue, and lack of self-worth (Arpin-Cribbie and Cribbie, 2007). ANTs need to be removed! Confidence Reforming Affirmative Beliefs (CRABs) that boost self-esteem and make us feel more positive need to be encouraged.

ANTs out, CRABs in!

Thinking points

Consider some of the factors that have boosted your confidence as a tutor.

The activity above was carried out with trainee teachers in the Lifelong Learning Sector and the following factors were identified. These correlate closely with the research by Norman and Hyland (2003). Confidence grew when:

- Practising teaching techniques and using their skills and knowledge in the classroom. Learning to relax and enjoy teaching, and realizing that nervousness is not unusual. Others felt the same.

- Positive feedback was received on their performance, and feeling secure about their abilities as the course progressed.
- Realizing they didn't need to know everything.
- Interacting socially with others to get help and advice, and working with other members of staff as part of a team. Being treated well and supported through tutorials and mentors.
- Familiarity was gained with the lesson materials and also receiving support and encouragement. Self-management improved, identifying areas to develop and engaging in action planning.
- Learning to cope with workload and constructive criticism to help improve performance.

Norman and Hyland (2003: 270) concluded that:

> the research indicated that although the individual learner can affect his/her own level of confidence, tutors, peers, mentors and workplace supervisors can help to increase the learner's confidence by providing support, encouragement and constructive feedback.

This highlights the importance for individuals to work on their self-esteem and confidence, but they also need the support and praise of significant others to make this effective. For example, this could be a mentor, a tutor, a colleague or one of the learners.

Thinking points

Think of a negative thought which stops you being confident. What would your ANT powder be to help remove it?

Taking action to help build your confidence

In this section, we provide ways to help build confidence and self-esteem. These are tips to help boost confidence and to look confident in the classroom, even when you don't feel it. Creativity in the classroom won't happen until confidence grows.

Be prepared

Try and be prepared for the class. We know this isn't possible all of the time, especially when a class has to be covered at the last minute. But preparation for timetabled sessions can certainly be organized. If a tutor enters a class with a lesson plan, familiar with the content and with plenty of learning materials, then confidence will rise immediately, as this will help him or her to feel relaxed and in control. Last minute planning, photocopiers not working, and poor classroom activities make the tutor anxious even before entering the classroom. In these circumstances, creative activities cannot be executed well.

Confident body language

The tutor needs to look confident, even if he or she doesn't feel it. The tutor is like an actor on the stage – whatever is happening outside the classroom needs to be left there, if possible, once they have walked through the door. Acting confidently will lead to feeling that way too. As Davies (2003: 50) says, 'One of the best ways to build confidence is to act as though you have it, even when you may not be feeling confident on the inside'.

Dressing the part is also important. Confidence grows when the clothes we are wearing feel comfortable and appropriate. So being well groomed and well dressed will help to present a confident front.

Thinking points

Consider the body language of a confident person and an unconfident person. Think about their posture, use of hands, facial expressions, their eye contact and voice.

Posture. Walk tall! Posture needs to be upright and open to indicate positive body language. Think of having a piece of string coming out of the top of your head making you feel tall, your back straight and head up. At the same time, you need to relax your shoulders and jaw muscles.

Use of hands. Fidgeting with hands often shows a sign of nervousness. If you can, try and film yourself teaching or ask for peer feedback. Do you tap your pen, or wave paper about? If you know you have a tendency to fidget, try to eliminate it!

Facial expressions. Friendly faces are important. Smiling shows confidence and creates a good first impression. Davies (2003: 51) says, 'To signal confidence, you need to ensure that your body language and facial expression are in harmony with what you are saying'. If the two do not match, a judgement will be made about the body language rather than what is being said, which can undermine the activity.

Eye contact. To build up rapport with the group, eye contact is vital. If the learners do not have this, they will feel that the tutor is distant and disengaging. Good eye contact suggests support and interest in the learners' contributions to the session. Some cultures regard eye contact as disrespectful, so be aware that this could be the case if the group is multicultural in make-up.

Voice and tone. To engage and enthuse learners, the voice is a vital tool. As well as speaking louder to project the voice across the room, pace and pitch are also important. A nervous speaker tends to talk quickly and with a higher pitch, so talk more slowly and lower to indicate confidence. Deep breaths can steady nerves, and a bottle of water to hand can be helpful if the throat feels dry.

The key to bringing learners on board with creative activities is to introduce enthusiasm and energy into the voice. This will encourage the learners to be enthusiastic and motivated too. A boring, monotone delivery is the best way to disengage learners and for them to lose their focus!

An important ground rule is to ensure everyone is listening before the tutor or a learner in the group speaks. Creative activities can have a great deal of class interaction and discussion. For this to work effectively, and for classroom management to be handled well, respect for others in the class and what they have to contribute is vitally important (see the section on ground rules in Chapter 5, 'Classroom Management and Creativity', p. 46). This important ground rule will demonstrate confidence and good management by the tutor.

The importance of constructive feedback for boosting confidence

Giving and receiving feedback is a valuable skill to be developed by both you as a tutor as well as for learners to aid their own and peer development. Wherever possible, feedback needs to be promoted in creative learning settings. When we are given a carefully thought through piece of feedback it is like a precious jewel, to be examined and valued. Feedback is especially important in respect of creativity. For the creative tutor, it provides data on the different approaches being adopted. The tutor may have invested a great deal of time and energy planning and executing a creative session or activity. Consequently, they will hope to ensure that the intended outcomes have been realized, and be aware of other unintended outcomes.

Relying purely on tutor perceptions may be problematic, as these may form only a snapshot of what occurred. Our notion of the 'space between' emphasizes the joint role of the learner and tutor in creating a learning experience. Therefore, gleaning feedback from learners on what they have gained from the creative session can be generative. This can be done informally – by careful observation and talking to learners – or using formal methods such as encouraging learners to write about (or build into presentations) their learning and the process through which it was obtained. Positive feedback will boost confidence in the tutor and learners. Constructive criticism that clearly indicates what was experienced, the problems associated with this and, vitally, how it could be improved will be seen as constructive and forward looking.

Learning from others

Using role models is a good way of building confidence. Observing other tutors who are confident using creative techniques with their learners can be extremely valuable. Try and seize an opportunity to observe or team teach with them to pick up useful tips and ideas to use with your own learners. Reflect on the way that they handle their groups and engage learners. Suggest that the tutor observes your lesson too. Having supportive and constructive feedback from others is a good confidence booster. If you are able to share creative ideas and resources with others, this is a great motivator and energizer too (see Chapter 10, 'Stimulating Creative Change in Your Practice', p. 126).

Working creatively with groups doesn't always go according to plan. Do not give up though. Reflect on the reasons why this has happened, as often it will be nothing to do with you. Could it be due to factors such as the time of day, a previous learning session with another tutor, unsuitable physical learning space, or the group dynamics? Can your creative approaches be adjusted to accommodate some of the problems faced? Often if you discuss issues with colleagues or a mentor, you will find they have the same concerns or did so in the past. If a strong team environment pervades, consider proactive strategies to find possible solutions.

It is important to keep these problems in perspective. As someone once said to one of the authors, 'At the end of the day, no one has died!' You can go into the next session and try something different. Reflect back on the situation with a sense of humour and learn from the experience. Nobody is perfect!

Looking after yourself

In this final section, we focus on nurturing the wellbeing of the creative self (see also Chapter 11, 'Looking after the Creative Tutor', p. 137). Confidence relates closely to your wellbeing and self-esteem. If your self-esteem is low, you are more liable to succumb to stress and lower the resistance of your immune system. This can also affect your ability to cope with everyday situations. Importantly, a burnt-out tutor who is lacking in confidence will be less likely to have the energy or inclination to be developmental and creative. Here are some tips to develop the positive you.

- Focus on positive situations that have occurred with your learners. Remember occasions when you have been praised and celebrated for the work you have done. This is good for building your learners' self-esteem and motivation too.
- Avoid negative self-talk. Don't put yourself down in front of peers or learners. Link up with others who provide a positive influence for you and limit your time with those who drain your energy and resources with their negative views.
- Maintain a work–life balance. It is important to give time to friends, family, and interests. Breaks from work recharge the batteries and allow you to have a clearer perspective on problems.
- Take breaks during the day. Even when snowed under with tasks, a few minutes away from the desk to grab a drink or a short walk outside will bring you back refreshed and more productive.
- Make a list of the tasks you need to accomplish, however small, and then cross them off once they are completed. This provides a great sense of achievement.

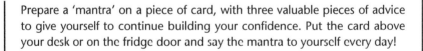

Thinking points

Prepare a 'mantra' on a piece of card, with three valuable pieces of advice to give yourself to continue building your confidence. Put the card above your desk or on the fridge door and say the mantra to yourself every day!

In summary, this chapter has addressed some of the issues that cause tutors to lack confidence in the classroom, and also those factors that can boost one's confidence. The key to confidence is building on the positive factors we have, through the praise and support of others, focusing on our good qualities, and realizing we are not alone and do not have to be perfect all the time. As confidence grows in the classroom, creativity will also increase. Creativity in learning settings concerns experimentation, withholding judgement, and doing things differently. That can be scary sometimes for both tutor and learners. If we wish our learners to go on that journey with us, they need to be assured their tutor is confident in intent, and has the skills to support them along the way.

The tips and suggestions offered here will help to develop confidence. It is important to prepare properly for lessons; to develop a positive body language with learners; to learn from others, especially those who are positive, supportive, and constructive in their feedback; and to look after yourself to build self-esteem.

All these tips apply to our learners too. Many of them are from diverse backgrounds, often having a 'second chance' in their education. They, too, may suffer from low self-esteem and negative thoughts. As tutors, it is important to praise them as much as possible, build up their confidence through support and constructive feedback, and encourage their engagement and motivation.

Activity: Confidence Quiz

Plot your confidence levels on a scale of 0 to 10 (where 0 = least confident and 10 = most confident) in the following categories:

1 **Meeting new people**
   How do you feel when you meet people for the
   first time?   _____
2 **Socially**
   Are you comfortable in social situations?   _____
3 **Professionally**
   Are you confident about the your level of qualifications
   and skills?   _____
4 **As a friend**
   Do you make and keep friends easily?   _____

(cont.)

(cont.)

 5 **Intellectually**
   Are you confident about your intellectual ability? _____

 6 **Your appearance**
   Are you happy about the way you look and present
   yourself? _____

 7 **Your fitness**
   Are you confident about your level of fitness? _____

 8 **Your coping ability**
   Are you able to cope in stressful situations? _____

 9 **Your talents**
   Do you have at least one special talent to offer? _____

10 **Your assertiveness**
   Do you feel your views and feelings are respected and
   taken into account? _____

11 **Capacity for enjoyment**
   How good do you feel about your capacity to enjoy
   yourself? _____

Look at the scores you have given yourself. This exercise helps you examine any areas where you may feel less confident, and what to concentrate on to make you feel overall a confident person.

There may be other categories you may want to add to this list, such as confidence as a parent or as a partner.

Part 2

The Group Perspective

Part 1 focuses on the creative individual tutor. It explores a state of mind we call 'mental space', which is closely linked to fostering creativity with learners. An important characteristic of this space is an enhanced sense of self-awareness on the part of the tutor. Such awareness is closely linked to a sense of competence – what is working well or not – and the ability to sense that a change of activity or approach is needed based on an assessment of the learning setting. Often LLS learners have diverse needs and require a tutor who inspires, encourages, and stimulates curiosity. Using a creative approach to teaching based on tutor self-awareness will help to engage learners.

Part 2 explores the nature of such engagement and presents different creative approaches that have enabled learning to take place across a wide range of LLS settings.

4 Introduction to Groups

The creative setting is a bounded space, where learners have the freedom to explore and experiment, while at the same time feeling supported and challenged. A tutor has responsibility for ensuring such a space is created. However, it is not their responsibility alone – learners also have responsibility for facilitating learning for themselves and their peers. Such dynamics make creative classrooms potentially exciting spaces, yet they also require skilled practice to make them effective.

This part of the book on group perspectives will explore the following areas:

- What social pedagogy is, and why this approach to education is so important to the Lifelong Learning Sector today.
- Working creatively with groups of learners, and what helps and hinders learners from being creative in those settings.
- Strategies tutors can use to enhance learning in groups, working with process as well as task requirements.
- The importance of providing learners with constructive feedback, praise, and recognition.

What is social pedagogy?

Social pedagogy is a holistic approach to education and development that recognizes the individual as a person in relation to others – their peers, their family, other groups and organizations that form part of their lives at any given moment.

> The work of the pedagogue is essentially personal ... the work of the pedagogue [is often spoken of] in terms of the human person: head, hands and heart – all three being essential for the work of pedagogy. The personal, relational approach is emphasised in students' training and education, where fostering sound pedagogic values and attitudes is seen as at least as important as the acquisition of knowledge and skills.
>
> (Petrie et al., 2009: 4)

Here learning and development is seen within its social context: consideration of the social environment in which it takes place. That immediate environment consists of the individual learner, their co-learners, and the tutor. Here the relationships and resulting interactions will guide the learning process.

In respect of the LLS learner context, however, we need to embrace the particular learning setting – a college, training unit, prison, workplace – as well as the socio-economic environment that exists for that learner, and others, at any one time. For example, the learning environment of a college learner in an area of high unemployment, in a socially deprived region of the country, will tend to be different from that of an employee attending a training course at a hotel outside a major thriving city. Aspirations, motivations, opportunities, and learning background are factors that impact on learning and development. Each learning setting will have different features separating it from others. Therefore, such differences need to be taken into account when discussing learning, motivation, and development.

The following principles of the social pedagogic approach, as adapted from Petrie et al. (2006), are linked to the Lifelong Learning Sector today:

- Focusing on the learner as a whole person and supporting the learner's overall development.
- The practitioner sees him or herself as a person in relationship with the learner.
- Tutors and learners are seen as inhabiting the same life space, not existing in separate hierarchical domains.
- As professionals, tutors are encouraged constantly to reflect on their practice and to apply both theoretical understandings and self-knowledge to the sometimes challenging demands with which they are confronted.
- Tutors are also practical, so their training prepares them to share in many aspects of learners' daily lives and activities.
- Learners' associative life is seen as an important resource; tutors should foster and make use of the group.
- There is an emphasis on teamwork and on valuing the contributions of others in relation to learners' learning, including other professionals, parents, and members of the local community.
- The relationship is central and allied to this is the importance of listening and communicating.

Why is this approach to education so important to the Lifelong Learning Sector today?

At one time, the demands of teaching in the Lifelong Learning Sector were mainly focused on getting the learners through the qualification or syllabus they were following. To some extent, this still holds. With ever increasing pressure for employment and entry to higher education, it is not surprising that tutors, and learners, feel pressured to ensure (literally) they make the grade. However, the increased diversity of learners as noted earlier, as well as the pressure on the Lifelong Learning Sector to accommodate the needs of young people and adults without employment, shifts attention to the needs of the individual learner. Social pedagogy is therefore suited to the needs of the Lifelong Learning Sector now and in the future. To help develop and support such learners, practitioners need to be attentive to the whole person: What makes them tick? What are their aspirations? How can the programme they are following fully embrace their particular learning needs? What feedback do they need to help them progress? Shoehorning a group of learners into a pre-packaged programme will not support the needs of such diverse learners.

Tutors need to recognize their practice as more than distributing knowledge in a variety of entertaining or engaging ways. Enabling the learner to explore values and attitudes to self and others, especially in an employment context, is critical within the LLS learning setting. For example, a recent news report on our local television station highlighted the plight of those who were seeking work in the construction industry. An 'open day' was shown where various employers and agencies were meeting prospective employees, both young people and adults, and offering advice and highlighting potential opportunities in the industry. The company representatives were in conventional business attire, mainly suits and smart clothes. However, most of the prospective candidates featured were in a variety of casual dress – plain jumpers, T-shirts, jeans or tracksuits, and baseball caps. Granted, this was not an interview, yet the event was still the first meeting of employer with prospective employee. Research on recruitment and selection indicates how important those first impressions are for a candidate to be successful. The Lifelong Learning Sector offers vital opportunities to learners for role-play and simulations to emphasize, and provide feedback on, appropriate business cultural norms, such as meeting with a decision-maker. Whether that is in a design class where a proposal is being pitched, a business enterprise course where a loan is being applied for with a bank, or the employment interview simulated within any course.

Too often, employability is seen as the responsibility of the careers and guidance staff who are brought in at a certain stage of the programme to 'deliver advice and guidance', often offering advice on filling in an application form or compiling a curriculum vitae. Developing employability skills needs to start on the first day of a vocational programme, with LLS tutors providing formative assessment to students on the development of their attitudes and skills, rather than its being seen as the responsibility of the careers or guidance unit.

Use of group work

Social pedagogy also contributes another important lens to understand learning and development in the Lifelong Learning Sector, through the use of group work in learning settings. Throughout the activities described in this text is a belief in the benefit of learners coming together in groups to discuss, model, challenge, and explore. Blatchford et al. (2003) draw on extensive research to develop a useful framework to examine group work at any one time. Moreover, the elements that comprise the framework are grounded in the social pedagogical approach to learning and development described above. The authors identify four elements of the framework:

1   *The learning setting*: preparing the learning setting and the groups
2   *Interactions between learners*: preparing and developing learners' skills
3   *The tutor's role*: preparing adults for working with groups
4   *Tasks*: preparing the learning session and group work activities.

First, Blatchford et al. recognize the importance of the learning space, and for the Lifelong Learning Sector this is crucial. For example, is it a standard classroom with possible flexible use of space, or a mechanics workshop with limitations imposed by health and safety or practical considerations? Each of these settings will not stop group work itself but will have a bearing on it. Overall group and individual group size is also important. The tutor has to be cautious about the size of groups and being able to manage a large number of groups at any one time. The composition of groups – gender, ability, background – also has to be considered. We stress throughout this part of the text that the learning space should not inhibit the tutor from considering creative approaches to learning. We recognize, however, that some spaces are more conducive than others. We provide examples of how rooms containing large groups or a technical workshop setting can still be used creatively to enable effective learning. (See Chapter 9, Creativity and Large Groups, page 111)

Second, by placing learners into groups tutors often assume that the learners know how to operate and learn within them. Groups develop, and learning will often not take place within them if group members lack trust and respect for fellow group members. In addition, groups need to be managed. So it is important that roles are assigned in groups – for timekeeping, note taking, leading, and presenting back – which allows the group to function effectively. Here there is valuable learning for individuals to be part of a group, to recognize the value of their contribution and the integrated nature of how a group can work. Ground rules (see Chapter 5, 'Classroom Management and Creativity', p. 46) are important for group work as much as other learning strategies in the LLS setting.

Third, the tutor needs to consider his or her ability to facilitate and guide groups. Good generic teaching skills are still applicable. Learners need to understand what the role of the group is within the wider learning objective of the session. The learning session also needs to have a form of briefing and plenary, to ensure integration of the whole group, as much as possible. We are not suggesting that every learning session needs a tidy ending in this precise form. Learning and learners are not like that. If the ending is intended to lead on to further work or development of the session, then this needs to be acknowledged, however ragged that 'edge' may be.

Learners also have to be supported and challenged if the tutor feels that the group is not working effectively. In other words, the tutor waits in the wings ready to intervene constructively and sensitively if they feel the group is veering off course. A good analogy is helping someone to ride a bike: the tutor doesn't pedal while the learners have their feet up on the cycle rack behind; rather, the tutor as facilitator acts to help the members back on their bike, and then provides a gentle shove of encouragement to get them on their way again.

Lastly, the task is a crucial factor in group working. The tutor needs to think through what the group is being asked to do:

- Does this task need a group setting?
- How can the particular group setting aid learning in this instance? Is the task suitably challenging for this group?
- Will it help exploration, discovery, analysis and synergy of ideas, thoughts, actions, for example?
- Does the group task need some individual or paired preparation, reflection or discussion first?

Such questions need to be addressed by tutors so as to prepare effectively for using groups in their learning setting. With group work, as with any other form of learning, the setting needs to be thought through before-hand in terms of task planning and preparation.

Group work and employability

When walking round many LLS organizations, a myriad of different learning spaces can be observed. From recognizable traditional classrooms with rows of desks facing forward to a screen, seminar or breakout rooms with small groups of desks, mechanical workshops or laboratories, to computer labs with individual workstations. The latter featured heavily in the programmes and magazine articles projecting what education (and workplaces) would look like in the twenty-first century. All of these learning spaces, however, have their place in enabling learning. The individual workstation, with information being conveyed between operator and machine, does not encourage communicating with, and working alongside, others.

Image reproduced with the permission of Azara Ayub

Employers frequently complain that new recruits have the technical skills required but lack the interpersonal skills that working together – whether with fellow employees or with customers – requires. Group work that is well facilitated enables learners to assess their capability in this area, as well as opens up the exciting possibility of co-learning alongside their peers. The chapters that follow offer plentiful examples of how employability skills are being fostered by creative learning approaches. Each example will clearly indicate the particular skills being developed.

5   Classroom Management and Creativity

Tutors in the Lifelong Learning Sector often raise issues to do with adopting creative methods of teaching, especially the impact on classroom management and dealing with any inappropriate learner behaviour that may result. One view expressed is that a more active learner has more scope to opt out of the task or disrupt others. Our position is different: working creatively with learners often fosters greater engagement and learning. The tutor may feel that didactic teaching brings about learning. Thus, having passive learners may fulfil a requirement for 'controlling' but are the learners learning anything? As Wenger (1998: 264) states, 'the relation between teaching and learning is not one of simple cause and effect'.

An assumption held by some is that the generic classroom management techniques tutors require, irrespective of teaching approach taken, are not relevant here, and the use of creative approaches involves a whole new way of working. Such an assumption is misplaced. Good classroom management is imperative when these methods are adopted, perhaps even more so. However, it will depend on individual circumstances:

- Is this the first time learners have experienced such methods? If this is the case, the tutor may need to be more directive in their approach and organize the session into shorter manageable chunks, rather than having longer periods of learner activity which they facilitate.
- Using the knowledge the tutor has of this group and sensitivity to the present context – sensing the mood of the group, the time of day, the nature of the task – the tutor needs to consider what is possible here in terms of creativity and the approach to be adopted. Here we see the creative tutor thinking on their feet and 'reflecting in action' (Schon, 1997).

Key elements of classroom management have been effective with groups of LLS learners. As practitioners working with a myriad of different learners in different LLS settings, we have identified the following as important in enabling learning through creative approaches.

Introduce ground rules

In Part 1, we discussed the idea of a creative space. There, space was described as taking three forms: physical, mental, and the 'space between' (see Chapter 1, 'Creative Learning Spaces', p. 12). The latter emphasized the relational nature of learning, that tutor and learner are involved in joint working, helping to define the relationship that is important for creative practice. Learners need to know what the boundaries of this space are. So ground rules help to determine what is acceptable and unacceptable within this space. Such boundaries act as a framework for operating within this space and, if built with contributions from the learners, the ground rules will be jointly owned.

To avoid the tutor imposing ground rules on the group, a process should be undertaken at the beginning of a programme or series of working sessions (such as a module) whereby the tutor asks learners what they consider to be acceptable behaviour and the conditions for enhancing learning in that space. Thus the learners are able to contribute rather than the rules being pre-packaged and delivered by the teacher. This is not a case of the tutor allowing learners a free rein; rather, the tutor encourages the learners to consider what they themselves think is appropriate to learn effectively. The resulting document can be distributed electronically, in paper form or as a class poster that is visible to all.

Ground rules are not set in stone but are a living 'contract' between tutor and learners, which as the learning process develops may need reinforcement, additions or greater clarity. Such practice recognizes the emergent nature of so much teaching and learning. Ground rules can become powerful tools in reinforcing and acknowledging positive behaviour and the resultant effects on learning. So the tutor can refer back to them and positively reinforce adherence during and at the end of sessions. Common ground rules that have featured in our creative spaces include classroom management issues of listening, respecting others, contributing to the best of ability, and asking questions if confused or stuck. An example of ground rules used with a group of adults training in creativity skills is shown below:

Ground rules for creativity

- Treat each other with respect.
- Listen and value others' opinions and contributions, even if they differ from your own.
- Contribute your ideas and thoughts.
- Be open to new ideas and approaches.
- Give constructive and supportive feedback.
- It is okay to make mistakes, we can reflect and learn from them.

Clear instructions

With student-centred learning (SCL), the tutor needs to ensure that instructions for learning activities are clearly communicated to the learners and that he or she provides the opportunity to clear up any confusion at the outset by checking with them that they understand what they are doing. If the learners are clear on this, there is less chance for disengagement. Often it helps to have the instructions on a PowerPoint slide so that the learners can refer to it throughout the activity. If this is not practical, another option is a copy of the instructions provided as a handout.

Being engaged and active offsets potential disruptiveness

When developing SCL techniques with LLS tutors, some participants express concern that student-centred learning results in loss of their 'control', which they find a bit scary. They believe this leads to learners 'doing their own thing', and some groups or individuals becoming disruptive or difficult to monitor.

Image reproduced with the permission of Azara Ayub

Once the tutors experience training in creative participative methods of teaching, they come to realize themselves that these methods engage students to a far greater extent than more didactic, tutor-led methods. Learning can be fun, enjoyable, and richer using these techniques. Increased engagement can lead to less disruptiveness, but it does mean that a different range of teaching skills has to be adopted. No longer does the 'tutor have to do everything'. This shift, with the emphasis firmly on 'learning', as opposed to 'didactic teaching', is difficult within more traditional systems of education, such as if LLS learners have been used to a diet of being 'taught at' throughout their previous learning experiences. Encouraging the learners to 'self-monitor' learning shifts the emphasis away from the belief that the tutor has to be didactic all the time.

A good illustration of the impact of a creative approach on a disruptive group is a tutor working in a British further education college with a group of twenty 16- to 18-year-olds studying on a Level 3 Business programme. Before they came to the tutor's session they had experienced a very didactic lesson from another member of staff, and three had been sent to see the Head of Department because of their disruptive behaviour. The tutor was anxious about how they might now behave in her own session. So she adopted a different learning approach. She divided the teenagers into four sub-groups. A different activity was assigned to each sub-group, linked to the requirements of the programme assessment. Resources were allocated with a range of learning materials: access to a laptop, articles, textbooks. Each sub-group then had a particular task to complete, such as writing letters, drawing mind-maps, and ranking information. There was evidence of more able learners supporting less able peers (how to use an index, for example). One of the previous lesson's most disruptive learners produced a visually intricate mind-map that astounded the tutor and his peers in terms of its quality, and how he responded to producing visual material, as opposed to reams of written text. The tutor found that at the end of this two-hour session she had to usher the group out of the room because they were not keen on curtailing the learning activity! On reflection, the tutor noted how the task set, and the student response, boosted their performance in the summative assessment that followed. This activity was based on the Learning Carousel in Eastwood et al. (2009: 42–3).

Preparation and pre-thinking

Invariably, good learning sessions come from effective planning, especially if the participants are doing something different in their practice – a view that could be applied to any teaching it might be assumed. However, adopting creative learning methods generates the need to think through and identify not only what the teacher is doing but also what the learner is going to be engaged in. More experienced tutors may be able to plan but then develop a learning situation that was unexpected or follow a train of thought that will result in rich learning for their learners. Schon (1997) describes this process as 'reflection in action' – the impromptu, a surprise pathway that enlivens and enriches learning. Inexperienced tutors may have yet to develop such skills. Planning becomes essential to help create the framework that guides the learners through the process and gives the session its structure. Such assurances may be especially important for encouraging less confident or less able learners, as they become more aware of session objectives and how well they are performing in respect of its planned outcomes. Again, as mentioned in the previous section, such learning strategies – the divergent or keeping to the plan – are decided by the tutor based on what is happening in the learning space at any one time. More experienced tutors have this sense. They are able to change pace and learning activity if learners are becoming disengaged or complete a task very quickly. Developing creative approaches to learning arms the tutor with a type of thinking and learning tools that can address such situations.

In conclusion, an assumption often held about creative approaches is that they lack the structure of more directive styles of teaching. This is not the case. More organization and thought have to go into the structure of a creative session, especially in respect of preparation. The learning rewards are far greater, however. Over time your resource bank of activities will build, so if a particular group does not seem to warm to an activity, you will have the ideas, activities, and teaching strategies to change it. Hopefully, you will build up a team of teaching colleagues who will add to this resource bank. Such collective endeavours both within and between organizations will be discussed in Chapter 10, 'Stimulating Creative Change in Your Practice' (p. 121).

Practical exercise: room layouts

The following exercise urges the tutor to consider three different room layouts, and to consider how the positioning of the tutor affects the engagement and monitoring of the learners in each one. The three room layouts are: the traditional style with desks in rows, the U-shape, and the bistro style arrangement.

Thinking points

Consider how the three room layouts below will benefit or hinder classroom management. What are the potential problems that could be faced? What strategies could be used to overcome them?

Sometimes there is little option as to how the room can be arranged due to fixed furniture, such as in a lab or a computer room. However, for some activities, chairs can be moved so that the room can be partially rearranged. Also, if circumstances allow, why not consider using the floor instead?

Layout 1: desks in rows

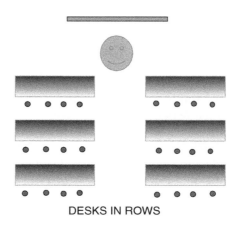

DESKS IN ROWS

Figure 5.1

The benefits

- All learners face the tutor and are able to see the whiteboard and screen.
- The tutor can see all the learners and can feel in control of the session.
- Easy to work both individually and in pairs.
- Avoids learners being distracted by others, as they are not in direct eye contact.
- Good use of floor space when teaching large groups.

The drawbacks

- Encourages more teacher-led sessions, as learners cannot work in groups as easily.
- Disruption caused to furniture and learners when organizing group activities.
- Learners experience difficulty moving around the room to work with different peers.
- Facilitation of activities is often more difficult for the tutor, as movement between the tables and the learners can be awkward.

- Discussions between tutor and learners tend to be public. One-to-one or small-group discussions are harder to organize in some parts of the room.
- Learners outside the tutor's eye-line are more likely to be overlooked and excluded from discussions.
- Poor behaviour, such as the prohibited use of mobile phones, can sometimes go undetected by the tutor, as learners at the back and sides of the room are not so clearly seen.

Strategies

- Organize where learners will sit before they enter the room to encourage working with others.
- Allow room for chairs to be turned around for group work.
- Clear spaces between tables to allow the tutor to move around the room.
- Consider teaching in another part of the room to make use of the wall space, or the floor area, for activities such as role-play.

Layout 2: the U-shape

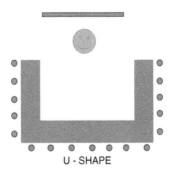

U - SHAPE

Figure 5.2

The benefits

- The tutor can see all the learners clearly.
- Better for participation in questioning, as everyone can see each other.
- Tutor can easily give one-to-one support to learners when working on activities, as movement around the centre is easy.
- Good for individual and pair work.
- Perfect for presentations, role-plays, discussions, debates, and demonstrations.

The drawbacks

- Learners on the side and corners have more difficulty seeing the whiteboard and screen. They always have to turn sideways to see the front of the room.
- As the focus is on the front of the room, it can encourage a more tutor-led session.
- Less confident learners can feel very exposed when being questioned.
- Learners tend not to mix with others on the opposite side of the room, but tend to limit their interaction with the person next to them.
- Disruptive learners can affect the concentration of the whole group.

Strategies

- Move chairs to inside the U-shape to encourage learners to work in groups more easily.
- Split the group randomly to encourage interaction and the sharing of new ideas with others not normally sat with.
- Often, a couple of tables can be moved without too much disruption to aid group work.
- Organize more role-play, debates, and group presentation activities.
- Facilitate small-group activities to reassure less confident learners.

Layout 3: the bistro-style arrangement

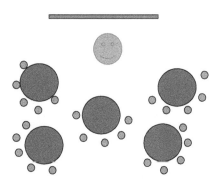

BISTRO STYLE

Figure 5.3

The benefits

- Good for small-group work and discussion.
- Easier for the tutor to move around the groups to facilitate student-centred activities.
- Encourages collaboration and teamwork between learners.
- Makes it easier to organize different learners to work together.
- Encourages more learner participation and contribution to the session.
- Better access allows the tutor to provide learners with one-to-one support and guidance.

The drawbacks

- Learners might have their backs to the tutor or other learners when they are speaking or contributing to the session.
- Learners may not be able to see the whiteboard or screen without sitting awkwardly. Not so suitable for tutor-led input.
- Disruptive learners on a table can distract others when working on individual activities or when they should be listening.
- The noise can increase dramatically when everyone is engaged in an activity.
- More space is needed when desks are arranged in this way. May not be possible for a large group.

Strategies

- Organize the chairs around the outside edges of the tables, which will help prevent the learners from having their backs to others.
- Plan the seating so that disruptive learners are separated from their friends.
- Organize the groups into mixed abilities, or into specialist sets depending on the activity.
- Set strict ground rules for talking. A buzz in the room is great for creating a relaxed, friendly atmosphere with groups of motivated learners. But the learners need to know when to curb the volume if it is disruptive to others. Always insist on no talking, but listening, when others are feeding back or contributing to the session.
- If room space is a problem, encourage the learners to turn their chairs to face others when working in groups.

During a session, the tutor may wish to use a variety of different teaching methods, and thus the layout of the space is an important factor. As

Powell (1997: 122) comments: 'this selection of activities will make huge demands on the organizational skills of the teacher, and if the use of IT and practical activity is added to the list then you begin to realize the importance of classroom layout'.

If there is an option to alter the room layout before the session starts, consider the best one to support the activities planned and to help learning.

In conclusion, this chapter has discussed the impact on classroom management when adopting creative methods of teaching. Many tutors think that inappropriate learner behaviour may result from running a creative session, as the tutor does not have 'control' over the learners. We have argued that when creative methods are applied, learners can be much more engaged and motivated, and the opposite is true. But, for these sessions to be successful, good classroom management is essential, and clear ground rules have to be set at the start. Ways to apply these to a creative session have been investigated, and also the impact of different room layouts on these approaches.

6 The Hooks of Engagement: Creative Methods to Engage Learners

Hooks: 'a musical or lyrical phrase that stands out and is easily remembered'.
(Monaco and Riordan, 1980: 178, cited in Burns, 1987)

In memorable songs, there is usually a 'hook' – a riff, a single sound, a lyric or a rhythm – that repeats and grabs our attention. The power of hooks is that they hold our attention for days after first hearing, often playing in the listener's head with pleasurable – or, occasionally, annoying – feelings attached! Effective hooks depend on good timing, so how the notes combine with 'spaces between' (that phrase again) allows the listener to be 'hooked' and engaged. There is simplicity about many effective hooks that cause them to remain, for some of us, for the rest of our lives.

The task for the creative tutor is how we use the concept of the hook, as described, to foster engagement with our learners. The qualities of a good hook can easily be transferred to a learning setting. The learning experience needs to endure beyond the session itself, and how we engage needs to be discernible and not cause confusion. Just as in the discussion earlier of the trainee saturating his peers with energy and enthusiasm to the extent that he felt de-energized, we do not wish the hook to be so drawn out that it becomes the session. There needs to be 'space between', to ensure that the learners can engage and employ their own sense-making (see Chapter 1, 'Creative Learning Spaces', p. 12).

To some extent, the idea of a learner being hooked suggests a deception – bait being dangled in front of learners that they are blindly attracted to, and then 'reeled in'. Not much scope there for personal choice and student-centredness. Our belief, however, is that creative teaching approaches will need to be employed to engage and motivate an increasingly diverse learner population. The hooks are the starting points for fostering engagement. As Ken Robinson has noted, we live in a most intensely stimulating period, what with the Internet, myriad of gadgets to access it, hundreds of TV channels, video games, and powerful forms of advertising utilizing all these platforms (Robinson, 2010). By comparison,

LLS learning spaces lack such stimulation. It is not surprising that learners switch off and turn their back on learning. We recognize that learning takes part in a context, and many systemic factors impact on learners in addition to the learning space created by tutors. Robinson speaks of the anaesthetic that is modern-day education, putting learning to sleep. He thinks that we should 'not be putting them to sleep ... but waking them up to what they have inside of themselves'.

Hook 'em using narrative

Before a session, it is important to think through how the proposed learning objectives can be attained, and how the learners will be engaged in them. Could it be a particular story that can be told? The classic Ken Loach film *Kes* has a memorable scene where Billy, the young pupil, tells the class of his wonder at the kestrel he trains. His natural and impromptu performance staggers his teacher and the rest of the class.

Narrative is a powerful tool – as long as it is relevant. It can also transcend cultures. One of the authors recently told a tale from his early teaching experience to a group of Chinese vocational tutors. The story focused on a trip organized for a group of 17-year-old students to a local factory in the UK to gain understanding of the manufacturing process and workings of the business. The story hinged on the plight of the tutor coping with his poor planning for the visit and the lack of interest on the part of the students. The Chinese tutors listened carefully and then shared their own experiences of such learner behaviour. The session moved on to look at how such visits can be effective but need learner involvement before the visit commences, careful planning with the host business, and then follow-up preferably led by the learner group. The 'hook', the story, prompted the richness of the outcomes for the Chinese learners. It acted as a reference point for them to add their own experiences, to foster humour and fun in the session – many of the issues were common across the two cultures – and to serve as a benchmark for how things could be different. This example is developed more fully as a case study in Chapter 7, 'Encouraging Constructive Thinking and Exploration of Ideas' (p. 75).

Just as in the film *Kes* learners themselves generate some of the most powerful stories. Encouraging learners to consider their own experience, make sense of it, and then present to the rest of the group can be a valuable learning experience for themselves and their peers. Some less confident learners may need prompting, and it is important that the rest of the group show respect to the story being told. Displaying regard for others is part of the respectful and open culture that the tutor needs to create in the session, so that these practices become part of how the individual engages with him or herself, through self-reflection, with others, and with the tutor. Again, it is sending a clear message to the group that it is not always the tutor's story that counts, since others' experiences can be valuable and relevant too.

Thinking points

If you have learners that lack confidence, consider getting them to make or use finger puppets or face masks. Often, telling their stories through a prop can be a lot easier for them. (See Chapter 9, 'Designing a Creative Session', p. 99.)

Hook 'em using music

Other creative forms can be used as hooks. Not all learners will be captivated by a story; others may be engaged through music or images.

The power of music to engage is evidenced by the advertising industry. The music accompanying adverts often alerts us to the particular brand and is designed to evoke emotions that we then attach to that brand. A well-known brand of cigar used Bach's 'Air on the G String' to suggest the languid pleasure of smoking in the days when such TV advertising was permissible. Hearing that music stimulates the image of that particular brand. Similarly, great film soundtracks act as sonic labels, denoting that particular film. The use of Ennio Morricone's soundtracks to the films of the Spaghetti Western genre is a good example. So music is a powerful tool when wanting to grab attention or express a particular mood. In Chapter 9, 'Designing a Creative Session' (p. 92), we discuss the use of music before a session starts as well as how music may be used as a timer to alert learners that the session is nearing its end.

Using music with learners can be tricky, however. The authors have experienced how background music can effectively hook particular learners as an aid to group or individual work (for further discussion, see Chapter 9, 'Designing a Creative Session', p. 92), or as part of a presentation by tutors or learners. On one occasion with a new group, the learners discovered one of their peers was a champion accordion player. So they encouraged her to play the instrument for a presentation, a component of their programme's assessment. The presentation involved a group task, so while the groups were engaged in the activity, the musician accompanied them with suitable tunes that fitted the task. Suddenly, the activity took on extra meaning as the music accompanied the action.

It is important to realize that music must not intrude on learning, but support it. Thus if the group is reflecting, the music must be quieter and more soulful. In contrast, if the group needs energy, the music should reflect the 'beat' of the activity. Using music can also backfire. The tutor may be a great fan of a band or artist but their passionate and biased choice of music could alienate the group they are working with. The increasing diversity of musical styles means that learners may be marginalized by certain choices made by the tutor, thus creating an unnecessary barrier. In this way, the use of music may backfire as a creative hook. Classical music can often be the obvious candidate when choosing suitable music but the increasing number of musical forms, including world music, can aid the recognition and value of the diversity of learners in particular settings (Eastwood et al., 2009: 84–5). Rap and hip-hop lyrics have been used to engage and motivate learners with poor literacy, with learners then embarking on creative writing tasks using these compositional techniques.

The use of music, therefore, needs careful thought. Whenever possible, learners need to be encouraged to use their own music, to take responsibility for hooks that engage them. Enabling learners to talk about their passion, whether it is the pupil in the film *Kes* or a learner explaining why a piece of music is so effective for *him or her*, engages and boosts learner confidence.

Thinking points

Consider the learning settings you work in. How might you introduce music to help engage your learners? Which music would you use to energize or enable reflection?

Hook 'em using images

Many learners, especially those that favour a more visual learning style, are likely to be hooked by images. The use of a powerful image to convey meaning, to stimulate discussion and inquiry, or to reinforce learning, can grab the learner's attention and solidify understanding.

Here are two ways to work with images:

1   The tutor can present an image – a photograph, drawing, diagram – and use it as an initial vehicle for exploring ideas or links between different components of those concepts (see Figure 6.1).
2   Alternatively, the group can assemble their own images, either spontaneously or be invited to collect images and bring them to the session.

This second option can be especially effective – it gives responsibility to the learner to stimulate interest, offers the opportunity for them to engage in individual work, or share and look for patterns in images chosen as part of small-group work. Moreover, they take ownership of their images – images chosen by them, not by their tutor. If the images are chosen before the session, the learning process has been sparked. Choices can be made as to which image is preferred over another. The tutor can use this choice-making as a useful learning tool by questioning the learners as to what different images they considered, which criteria they used, and why some were chosen and not others.

Figure 6.1 shows a collection of different models and artifacts that a group of learners have assembled while carrying out a variety of creative tasks. The tutor is about to start the same programme with a new group of learners. There is also the danger when using creative approaches that

Figure 6.1 Collection of learners' creative learning tools

some learners may look for shortcuts by using the ideas of others rather than developing their own. Therefore, it may not be in the tutor's interest to pass around models or other similar artifacts made by previous groups. Thus the tutor should present the image in Figure 6.1 as depicting the end product of a learning activity, and that these are the types of artifacts that this new group is capable of producing.

The following are ways in which the image could be used as the hook:

- The group could be required to complete examples of such creative learning tools, the tutor using the image as a 'way in' to engage the learners, rather than just talking about the tools (for further discussion, see Chapter 9, 'Designing a Creative Session', p. 92).
- Examples of objects could be passed around the group as they are describing them.
- The learners might be set an initial task before the tutor discloses what the image contains. For example, the individual/group could guess what each of the objects could be used for (see Chapter 9, 'Designing a Creative Session', p. 100).
- The learners could assemble questions to ask about the different tools as presented by this image.

All the time the tutor will be using the image to build curiosity, hold attention, and help sense-making.

Not all images have to be so pre-packaged. A 'staple activity' of one of the authors has been the use of the collage. Over time, a collection of images from magazines of all types – supplements of newspapers, music magazines, etc. – as well as from newspaper advertisements is assembled. When seeking an affective response to a topic or concept, the learners are encouraged to pick out an image or a number of images that seem to connect with their thoughts and feelings. In sub-groups they are encouraged to talk to their peers about the images they have selected, and how they made connections with the theme. The sub-groups can then decide which of the images presented excited or inspired curiosity. The individual or pairs chosen by the group can then present their sense-making to the whole group. It is important to stress that each image chosen is personal to the learner concerned. Therefore, there is no 'best' overall image with an associated 'prize'. The use of competitive criteria can exclude and demean the individual's sense-making. The aim of the exercise is to do the opposite. It seeks to honour the individual's creativity in seeing divergent connections between the theme/concept and the image. A derivation of this activity is to encourage the learner to seek out for themselves, between sessions, an image that sums up for them the learning they have gained, or a question that still remains for them that they wish to explore further at the start of the next session.

Discussing official policy on the use of mobile phones by learners can use up many hours of tutor meetings. Not all countries' educational systems are so strict. Recently, while teaching in a foreign country with a group of university tutors as participants, the authors were astounded to observe phone calls being taken and made during the session. One thing is clear – phones aren't what they used to be! The power and potential of contemporary devices is immense. Learners' phones can be harnessed in a positive learning environment to encourage feedback, recognition of achievement, and research. For example, learners can be encouraged to take a photo of a particular artifact they may have produced: this could be a mind-map or a physical model, a presentation or picture of a sub-group. The resulting photo can be shared among the sub-group as a record of their achievement, or the image of the artifact used for further analysis or reflection. A word of caution: there are risks with the use of camera phones in learning spaces, such as inappropriate or offensive images being taken and shared by learners. Strict ground rules will need to be in place regarding such potential behaviour, with any image-sharing checked out with all members of groups and permission granted. In addition, some institutions may have strict policies regarding phone use and creative tutors will come under pressure to abide by these.

Hook 'em using moving images

YouTube, the video-sharing website, is a global phenomenon. In 2010, it had two billion views of its content a day. In 2011, this grew to three billion, until finally, in 2012, four billion videos were streamed each day. Sixty hours are uploaded each minute (Oreskovic, 2012)! The rise also of 'vlogs' – video blogs, whereby viewers subscribe to a channel – has made some of the contributors as famous as more conventional celebrities on terrestrial TV. Such moving images are popular through being personal and interactive. If someone is vlogging, then the viewer can instantly contact that person, unlike TV celebrities, who remain remote and detached from the viewer. Many learners are incredibly animated by moving images. Just overhearing conversations the next day after a torrid episode of a TV soap opera proves that the most reserved learner in a group will display surprising powers of expression and levels of engagement. Thus if these forms of moving images are so powerful, how might the creative tutor use the same process inside, and outside of, the conventional learning space?

The most common mistake made by tutors using moving images is to use too much material at any one time. Often the selected material does not have the excitement of a half-hour soap opera episode, or the visual and vocal appeal of a music video. Not all learners have a long attention span, so keep the extracts short and encourage the learners to interact with what is being shown. A sequence of ten-minute clips followed by buzz groups, in which learners share ideas, pose questions or write down reflective thoughts, is far more productive than a fifty-minute screening with a short discussion before the end of the session. Encourage learners to make and share videos of their own. Camera phones often have a perfectly adequate resolution for using video in the learning space. For example, partners can be encouraged to interview each other about a facet of their learning, and then selected interviews can be used with the whole group for review. If a learner has produced a really good artifact of some form, a model, a piece of written work, or has a rich experience on work placement, for example, ask them to video themselves talking about it. With permission, the tutor can then relay that to other members of the group, and encourage them to consider what is being said, and how it may match their own learning. Experiences captured in this way can be rich sources of recognition for learners. A word of caution: some learners may be highly conscious of how they appear or sound on screen, so the tutor has to be sensitive to this.

Using moving images outside of the conventional space can also be generative. The tutor may ask the learners to research a topic before they begin studying it, by selecting a video clip to present to other members of the group. An adaptation of this activity is where a group can contribute to a wiki. Each learner uses software to compile his or her own wiki using a mix of written and visual material. Other learners then view the pages and add their own contributions, so the group edits a series of shared pages (see Eastwood et al., 2009: 100).

Insights gained from moving images do not always have to be shared. The learner may be encouraged to write about their selected clip, explore why it was chosen, what is significant about it, and what else they would like to know about the subject matter.

Finding ways to engage LLS learners can often be challenging. Nevertheless, the tutor is required to make learning engaging and developmental. That is unlikely to occur if learners are faced with new experiences that look and sound very much like those they have witnessed before. Through appropriate hooks using narrative, music or images, the learner is drawn into a learning environment that is different, stimulating, and suited to different learning styles. Moreover, by providing creative opportunities as often as possible for learners to consider what 'hooks them', the tutor will ignite the process of learner responsibility and reap dividends for both tutor and learners as the programme progresses.

7 Encouraging Constructive Thinking and Exploration of Ideas

In an age of learning that has been battered by the rise of the inspection and cost culture in many LLS organizations, the importance of cultivating creativity has never been greater. Embedded in many arts and humanities programmes in schools and colleges is a way of thinking, developed through education and learning, of how to encourage innovation and creativity. Moreover, technical and scientific education has a strong problem-solving and idea-generation ethos underpinning exploration and invention. In the Lifelong Learning Sector, we have the opportunity to combine these different subject traditions to engender greater learner engagement.

Creativity is not a marginal activity. Through encouraging learners to explore, imagine, and problem solve, the Lifelong Learning Sector can enable further development, change, and enhanced employability. Figure 7.1 depicts the components of learners as active inquirers. In the section that follows, each component is explained in relation to the LLS context.

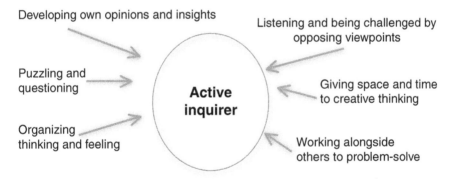

Figure 7.1 Characteristics of an active inquirer

Active inquirers, not passive sponges

How can we use creative methods in a group setting to help students think constructively? Problem-solving is part of this process but being able to think constructively is a far more useful tool. Here, the problem is framed as a search for a way forward, the generation of options; the discussion of what is possible within particular settings. As tutors, however, it is important to create spaces that allow time for creative thinking. It might appear easier to fill in gaps in thinking and do the learners' work for them (especially if feeling pressured to 'get through the syllabus'). However, these would be the tutor's insights and not those of the learners, thus denying them the opportunity to develop skills of independent thinking and opinion.

Moreover, it is unreasonable to expect learners simply to form groups and then be given problems to solve. Working in groups in this way is not just about cognitive reasoning but also the expression of feeling and emotion. Learners in the Lifelong Learning Sector often have rich life experiences that a skilled tutor should encourage to be shared and used to gain insight and further learning. Such experiences rarely are devoid of emotions – excitement, disappointment, anger, agitation – and within these heightened feelings are the keys to engage others and persuade. The tutor has a responsibility to help try and organize such thoughts and feelings through how the groups are formed, the operation of ground rules within the learning space, as well as encouraging learners to have a passion and then engage with others. Groups working in creative spaces offer many opportunities to individual learners to develop these skills.

The next section offers three examples of how activities can be designed and operated in an attempt to bring about active inquiry by learners. In addition, the benefits and drawbacks of each activity are described, together with follow-up activities where applicable.

1 *Stimulating constructive thinking: the Sticky Notes Scorecard Activity.* In the first example, the use of the learning space and the resources within the group are to the fore. Also, individual reflection, group activity, and whole-group exploration are important.

2 *Effective listening and engaging with difference: the Glasses Activity.* Being able to listen effectively and challenging – and being challenged by – opposing viewpoints are further elements that help LLS learners to be creative and innovative. This fun activity is designed to engage learners in developing their listening skills, assembling arguments, and working with the resulting dialogue.

3 *Puzzling and questioning: the Foundry Visit Case Study.* It can be testing for a tutor to encourage learners, with limited life experience, to puzzle about and question subject areas. This activity seeks to use a creative case study approach to help learners pose questions and offer suggestions for improvement to the tutor. In addition, what makes a 'good' creative case study is also addressed.

Stimulating constructive thinking: the Sticky Notes Scorecard Activity

A group was undertaking a programme with nine key principles. The tutor was keen to determine, part way through the programme, how well individuals in the group understood the principles. The tutor thus designed the following activity.

1   The tutor ascertained that there were nine key principles the group needed to understand at this stage of their programme.
2   Before the learners arrived, the tutor wrote '1' to '9' on nine separate sheets of paper and positioned these on the four walls of the room, evenly spaced.
3   Using a PowerPoint slide that diagrammatically displayed the principles, the tutor briefly explained each principle in turn.
4   The learners were told that each numbered sheet of paper represented a principle, as seen on the PowerPoint slide.
5   The tutor then handed out two sticky notes to each learner. On both sticky notes they were asked to write their name.
6   The group members were then asked to decide which of the nine principles they understood the best. They were asked to go to that numbered sheet and place their sticky note to the left of that sheet.
7   The group members were then asked to decide which of the nine principles they understood the least. They were asked to go to that numbered sheet and place their remaining sticky note to the right of that sheet.
8   There were clusters of sticky notes adjacent to certain numbers – some evenly matched between left and right sides of the principle, others more to one side. The latter indicated that most learners understood or did not understand that principle well, depending on which side of the sheet the cluster of notes appeared. In addition, very few sticky notes appeared to the left or right of some sheets.

It would have been easy at this point for the tutor to jump in and try and interpret what all this meant for group understanding of the nine principles. However, an alternative was to ask the learners:

- What did they notice?
- What trends could they see?

- What might this mean in terms of shared understanding (as the learners perceived it)?
- How might the group gain a greater understanding of the nine principles?

By doing this, the tutor was getting the group to question, to generate tentative conclusions from the displayed data, to formulate an idea of where they stood, both as an individual and as a group, in terms of understanding. The tutor was able to fill in gaps if she felt the group was not generating enough ideas, or stimulate further inquiry with her own questions directed to the group.

Follow-up activities

A follow-up activity was connected to the fact that each of the sticky notes had a name on it. Some sheets had a lot of sticky notes to the right but also some to the left. The learners formed breakout groups with a mix of left and right, and those with a sticky note to the right were encouraged to describe why they were having problems in understanding that principle. Those with a sticky note to the left were able to help their peers secure a better understanding of that particular principle. Groups of two or three could be organized, using the same emphasis on dialogue, with one side coaching the other.

As mentioned above, the resulting learning space is a snapshot of the group's understanding part way through a programme. Continuing the photographic metaphor, the tutor and learners could capture the group's understanding by taking photographs of each of the nine sheets. The tutor could do this or give the learners responsibility using their camera phones. Towards the end of a programme, these pictures can be revisited to see how understanding has changed. Has understanding improved with a shift of sticky notes from the right to the left of each principle? Or has understanding decreased, with a shift from left to right?

As a review task before an assessment, for example, the tutor could ask the learners to form sub-groups of 'left-handers' to present their understanding of a particular principle. This would help recap the principles and reassert ideas from earlier in the programme. Not all learners are blessed with high self-esteem, so if the tutor is to recognize effort and understanding by offering praise, where it is due, the confidence of the learners will be boosted before an assessment or test of their knowledge.

This particular activity was used for a programme of study. It could be used in a variety of different learning contexts, however, such as when a tutor wants the group to engage in different levels of reflection of a concept or problem. The latter could be broken down into constituent parts, each part being given a number and the left-hand and right-hand side used for questions, solutions, advantages and disadvantages, or examples. The breakout activities would also still hold. Sub-groups could be formed around particular numbers, or types of problems identified and solutions offered. Further inquiry could then commence within those groupings.

The benefits

- It encourages use of the whole learning space. The focus is not to the front, where the tutor may stand, but around the whole space.
- Learners are encouraged to move around and not be passive. This generates energy in the room.
- The activity encourages thinking about progress of the self as well as the whole group – formative self-assessment and peer assessment.
- Gives responsibility to the learner and the group as a whole to review the programme to date.
- It is a balanced scorecard. The activity highlights strengths as well as areas the group needs to develop.
- The room is a visual representation of progress and work still needing to be done. Providing an opportunity for the tutor to encourage dialogue around learning. In addition, the activity results in a snapshot for the tutor of what they have achieved but also what they need to do to increase understanding.
- Learners can target certain principles for further thought and greater understanding, which aids action planning.
- Tutors can point to evidence of how the group is progressing, both in terms of what they see as strengths and their ability to pick out areas for development. It provides an opportunity to *praise the group* both on their achievements to date and on the ideas they have generated to help them move forward.
- It provides the tutor with a snapshot of what they themselves have achieved, and also insight into what they need to do to increase understanding.

The drawbacks

A caveat to the above is that the learners make their decisions based on what *they think they understand*. A learner may believe they understand the principle but it could be that they are actually way off the mark. One way to check understanding is for the tutor to invite a range of learners to stand to one side of a number and explain to the group why they placed their sticky note where they did. The tutor and the remaining group members can listen to their explanation and check whether it is an accurate understanding of that principle or not. The tutor can then intervene, or invite other group members to do so, and provide the correct explanation of that principle if need be.

A further drawback of the Sticky Notes Activity is that it only enables the group to identify two of the principles. In other words, it deals with extremes of understanding: what is best and least understood. What about the other seven principles? It could be that these will be covered by the resulting exploration but there is no guarantee that that will be the case. An adaptation of the activity would be for it to be done in groups where learners rank in order their degree of understanding. However, although more discussion may take place within this setting across all the principles, the whole-group setting of the activity will be lost.

The activity was designed originally for use at the midway point of the programme, as a means of evaluation. The tutor and learner, at this stage, may only require a 'snapshot' of learning and understanding. The original design, therefore, enables areas of success and major difficulty to be identified.

In conclusion, the activity above illustrates how learners can be encouraged to question, but within a structured creative process. The aim is to stimulate constructive thinking. Part way through a programme, some learners have little idea what they have learnt and no conception of what needs to be thought more about and developed. The balanced scorecard emphasizes the process of learners taking responsibility for thinking more deeply about their progress. Moreover, the activity is an illustration of how learners may achieve this. Rather than a purely self-reflective activity, or a question-and-answer tutor-dominated review session, learners are actively engaged in large or small groups, or pairs, to investigate the idea being presented. Crucially, the tutor guides this process and only intervenes when necessary. Such facilitation helps learners engage with the subject matter, and so encourages self and peer formative assessment. Finally, the whole physical space is employed to enable this to happen. (The use of sticky notes is also discussed in starting a lesson and in giving feedback in Chapter 9, 'Designing a Creative Session', p. 94.)

Effective listening and engaging with difference: the Glasses Activity

Constructive thinking is one component of fostering active inquiry in learners. Being able to listen effectively and to challenge, and be challenged by, opposing viewpoints, are further elements that help our learners to be creative and innovative. There is a tendency to be drawn to those views that support our own. Newspapers are favoured that support our own world-view, or music that we have always favoured is forever bought and played. To explore difference and fresh ideas is enriching – it breaks the cycle of familiarity and encourages lateral thinking. Moreover, it sends a clear message to learners that creativity is related to a set of skills that can be learnt. In so doing, it challenges the views that learners sometimes express that only some are creative, certain subjects are 'creative' or 'non-creative', and that learners need to be inspired to embark on creativity.

Furthermore, when learners are employed in the workplace, the ability not to rush to a solution to a problem but to listen to those around them, without prejudice, is a vital skill.

Learners also need to recognize how important effective listening is to their own development. If they receive constructive feedback but decide to hear only half of what is said, the good parts or the areas for consideration, then development may be hampered.

So, what sorts of approaches can be employed in LLS learning spaces to encourage such practice? Again, we begin from the same starting point: to decide upon an activity that engages, as well as being fun and developmental.

The following activity helps the learner to actively listen to a viewpoint and then recognize and engage with the opposing arguments. Props are used in the form of 'glasses' made from pipe cleaners (Figure 7.2; see Chapter 9, 'Designing a Creative Session', p. 100). The making of these often generates much laughter as particular colours and shapes are used to rival even the best designer shades! These handsome creations enable, in this activity, the wearer to see a situation or person through a particular lens, or within a certain perceptive framework. This approach is based on the reflective model of Brookfield's Lenses (Brookfield, 1995), where events are viewed through different 'eyes': from the tutor's own perspective, from the learner's viewpoint, from that of their peers, and from a theoretical stance.

The subject matter here is barriers to learning and the strategies to overcome them, but any subject matter with different viewpoints or positions could be used. The learners in the activity below were Business and Technical Education tutors. The activity was part of a programme designed to develop student-centred teaching methods. The learners, however, could also be employees dealing with customers, managers working alongside other employees, or carers and their clients. In other words, any situation in which there are different perspectives on a shared life context can be chosen as the subject matter for this activity.

The activity was designed as follows:

1   The tutor invites the whole group to take part in a simulation activity.

Figure 7.2 Using pipe cleaner glasses

2   The learners have to consider the groups or individuals they are likely to be teaching.
3   Individual learners then reflect on the following questions: (a) 'What barriers do you think your students will come up against that may prevent them learning effectively?' (b) 'In your role as their teacher, what possible strategies could you use to help to reduce the effects of these barriers or prevent the difficulties occurring?'
4   The learners form groups of four (or more dependent on the size of the total group).
5   Within these groups the learners are to share the results of their brainstorm and pick two barriers and decide upon two strategies to overcome them. (This is based on 'Headaches and Aspirins' in Eastwood et al., 2009: 98.)
6   Glasses are then constructed out of the pipe cleaners provided.

7   Two members of the group are chosen as the learners with the barriers to learning. These two members put on their 'learner glasses'. They have the following written instructions: 'Now explain to the other members of your group, your "tutors", what the problems are, what happens when you try to learn, and what the consequences are for you of not being able to learn effectively.'

8   The 'tutors' – the remaining members of the group – listen to 'their learners' talk about the two problems. They put on their 'tutor glasses'. The 'tutors' have the following written instructions: 'Now explain to your learners what you are going to do to help reduce these barriers to learning. Remember to refer to the key principles of student-centred learning. Which ones apply here do you think?'

9   The groups then reflect on their learning about effective listening and dealing with challenging viewpoints. Key questions could include:

   • What helped and hindered your ability to listen to the other group members?
   • What enabled you to respond effectively to a challenging viewpoint?
   • Consider how you can apply these skills in your own workplace and with whom. When might be the next opportunity? Who might be able to give you feedback?
   • From this activity, what have you learnt about how this relationship might be different?

To avoid the monotony of each group feeding back similar points, it is better to have each group reflect on a particular question or part of it. So one group may feed back on help to listen effectively, another on responding effectively, and so on. Such a focus helps the groups to remain engaged and potentially increases the depth of reflection that they may be involved in.

The benefits

   • Learners who have taken part in this activity often mention the fun element of constructing and then wearing the glasses to get into role.
   • The glasses act as an aid to get into role and help focus on the thoughts and feelings of that position.
   • The rule of the activity – that only when the glasses are worn can they then talk 'out of' that position – applies a structure to the

activity and stops different opposing viewpoints being shared at any one time.

- Taking on the role of 'the other' encourages learners to think through that position, instead of being wedded to their own and all its conclusions.
- The reflective questions focus on personal skills that enable understanding and working with different challenging positions.
- The emphasis on how things could be different in this relationship moves the position away from entrenchment to one of possibilities and taking action.
- Some learners will not have experience of workplaces. As long as they have sufficient briefing material, they can engage with work-based issues through simulation.

The drawbacks

- The material the groups have for discussion will be limited unless sufficient time is given over to considering the subtleties of the opposing viewpoints before the discussion takes place within the groups. So learners may lose interest and become disengaged.
- Rules need to be observed for the activity to flow and for learners to recognize the potential of this form of communication.
- Insufficient attention is paid to the skills of effective listening before the activity is launched. Checklists and guidance material need to be prepared to support learners, unless the activity is used as an experiential tool to raise students' awareness of 'how not to do it'.
- Without feedback from peer observers, or the tutor, the participants in the groups may be unaware of the particular subtleties of some of their behaviours while carrying out the activity. Gaining permission to film one of the groups engaged in the activity might be useful, to draw the attention of the whole group to the potential learning points generated by the activity.

De Bono (1995) describes the need to break out from traditional ways of thinking that he believes are far too adversarial and lock participants into positions that they cannot get out of. Such polarities he considers are often at the expense of wisdom. An alternative approach is to recognize the need for parallel thinking: laying ideas down side by side, possibly with old ideas to determine which is most useful. The trick, however, is not to pre-judge or get corralled into favouring one or the other. We need, according to de Bono, to take time to explore possibilities, the goals to be achieved, decide who needs to be involved, and which views need to be taken into consideration.

For LLS learners, such an approach is important. The world that young adults are to inhabit is becoming increasingly complex and un-certain – the rather anachronistic term 'lifelong learning' was coined more than a decade ago. It was felt that such learning throughout life would help young adults cope with the uncertainty and anxiety re-sulting from such shifts in economic and social realities. Some went further – for example, the RSA announced a Charter for the 21st Cen-tury that would provide young people with the opportunity not just to adapt to changing conditions in their life but be empowered to transform them (http://www.thersa.org/projects/past-projects/education-campaign/ education-for-the-21st-century-a-charter).

Changing economic realities since the financial collapse of 2008, how-ever, have led to more than one million young people in the UK not in education, employment or training. The discourse is much more an eco-nomic than an educational one – the quest is to get young people into work rather than raise the aspirations for learning of all young people and adults. Yet, employers still bemoan the lack of basic skills and interper-sonal skills of the new recruits they employ. The need for confident and innovative young people and adults has never been greater, both to benefit the organizations they work for and, equally important, the communities that they are a part of.

Bringing work into the creative classroom: the use of case studies

Working as a tutor in LLS can potentially mean working with a whole range of learners: old and young, males and females, professional and manual workers, specialists in arts or technical subjects, courses for lower level and higher level qualifications. As identified in Part 1 of this book, the key is to engage the group in front of the tutor, at any one time, as groups can change. A challenge can arise though: How do we encourage learners to explore and construct ideas if they lack basic experience, especially work experience?

As tutors gain experience, they assemble a bank of creative resources that they know have 'worked' with different groups. One common re- source to bring the world of work, or the 'outside world', into the learning space is the case study. There are many advantages to using case stud-ies: an opportunity for learners to understand a real-life scenario, to get together and discuss and analyse the puzzles and challenges it presents, then identify the learning and connection to what is already known. So, the case study intends to flesh out the abstract. But a word of caution, the subject matter needs to be relevant to the learner. One of the authors worked with a colleague in a college who was a massive Bob Dylan fan. All of his case studies had a title that was in some way linked to the work of the great musician, even though the case material did not reflect the heading at the top of the case study pack. The students did not share his enthusiasm, as few of them even knew who Bob Dylan was; the tutor had disengaged them from the start. He obviously gained a great deal from the creative machinations of linking the material to his knowledge of Dylan, but his learners had less pay-off.

Another tutor had a far more profitable approach. Faced with a learner who was totally disengaged, she was doing all she could to present material that was engaging and what she felt was relevant. Still, the learner remained impassive and withdrawn. The tutor tried another tactic. She listened carefully to the learner both inside and – when they could – outside of the learning space. The tutor noticed that the only time the learner became energized was when he was talking about his beloved football team, Manchester United. So the tutor changed tack, gave the learners the task of bringing their own examples of organizations they were familiar with: corner shops, McDonalds, a betting shop, a cricket team they played for, a night club, and for our reluctant learner, Manchester United. At the next class, the tutor was presented with this thick folder of material that the learner had assembled overnight, including the sponsor-strewn club shirt. The tutor immediately got the learner to talk about why he had chosen the various items and how they connected to what he had been learning in class. Now the learner recognized that one of the largest football teams in the world was also a complex organization, with all facets of business operating within it. Praise was given to the learner for his newfound enthusiasm and collation of the material. The tutor had found the learner's passion. The choice of case study was the learner's, not one imposed by the tutor. Consequently, the learner was engaged not only with his head but also his heart. He cared passionately about the football club. Now the tutor had helped him to become passionate about his learning.

Effectively told stories are useful tools, especially if they are relevant to learner study needs. The contrasting case studies above are communicated through a narrative that contains characters, a beginning, and an ending. Telling a powerful story may be enough to raise interest and galvanize learners to want to inquire more. The use of narrative, however, also provides opportunities for learners to be actively engaged beyond mere listening.

Puzzling and questioning: the Foundry Visit Case Study

This activity is based around a scenario of a group visiting a casting company. The tutor relates the story of the trip to small groups of learners who are required to answer questions about how the visit could have been made more successful. The following are the different steps in the activity.

1   Learners are asked to form groups. Each group has an envelope on the table in front of them, a different coloured pen, and a pack of sticky notes.

2   The envelope contains a particular task related to the story they are about to hear. For example, one group is to listen and note down all the health and safety questions they would wish to ask from listening to the story, while another is to list a set of questions for how the visit could have been made more successful.

3   The tutor relates the story (the following is a summary of that narrative). It comes from his personal experience of taking a group of young people to a nearby foundry on a course visit. The tutor had all good intentions – getting the group out of the classroom, giving them experience of a real-life business, as well as awareness of a dirty, noisy working environment. The visit does not go well. The contact at the firm fails to arrive, they are shown round by someone who has little understanding of what they want from the visit, the tutor realizes there are more dangerous hazards than he originally thought, and the group becomes distracted by the lewd remarks made by workers to female members of the group. The tutor ushers them through as quickly as possible to minimize the potential damage to both his reputation and his learners' welfare. The latter are disgruntled and tell the tutor that the visit had been a waste of time.

4   Once the tutor has told the story, the groups discuss their individual tasks, putting their resulting questions onto sticky notes.

5   Each group is asked to come and stick their notes on a wall. Once a group has finished putting their notes up, the next has to assemble theirs in such a way as to show links to the previous group's questions, or the question may just be stuck up alone.

6   The resulting contributions display a range of questions and also how certain aspects are linked together.

7   The tutor requests the groups to guess the wording on the task sheet in each envelope besides their own.

8   Finally, the tutor invites group members to offer their own insights into what the display suggests and what links they can see.

An alternative approach

Instead of using sticky notes, the members of the group take on the role of journalists from different trade magazines, representing the different facets of the story that were in the envelope. They then have to 'interview' the tutor at a 'press conference' with a set of prepared questions in their role of being employed by that journal. The learning space can be set up as a press conference with a member of the group acting as a chairperson next to the tutor, with different group representatives asking the questions, and the chairperson inviting the tutor to answer them. (This idea is also discussed when using props in Chapter 9, 'Designing a Creative Session', p. 100.)

Follow-up activity

The respective groups take away their questions and then research the answers to them. Or they can exchange questions with other groups and see if they can help them with the answers.

The groups draw a poster describing the learning from the activity in respect of either their particular focus or showing the interrelatedness of the questions across the groups.

The benefits

- The narrative is from the tutor's own experience, so has the potential to be told with sincerity and feeling, increasing the chances of engagement.
- Learners are invited to comment on the tutor's poor performance – dispelling myths of tutor superiority and being 'all-knowing'.
- Rather than the group as a whole merely listening, they have a separate task in sub-groups to ponder and complete. This helps focus group activity and provides the chance for learners to add comments to others contributions once they provide feedback – the snowballing effect of building on others ideas (Petty, 2009: 237–8).
- The quiz element at the end of trying to guess the wording in the envelope can inject fun and inter-group rivalry.
- Learners are encouraged not to give solutions but to raise questions about the story they are being told. Such an approach reinforces the creative potential of the story, subverting the tendency of quick-fire case study answers for a more quizzical, inquiring methodology.

The drawbacks

- More often than not, the power of a story is in the telling. The tutor needs to be able to make the narrative engaging. A dry rendition of a former experience is going to be less than helpful. Humour, in the form of poetic licence to make the story more engaging for the particular group the tutor is working with (the detail of tubs of molten metal swinging through the air and the stench of casting make for great dramatic potential!), can enhance learner appeal.
- The story needs to be relevant. Just as in the Bob Dylan example above, the tutor may find the narrative enthralling but trying to shoehorn material to fit an unrelated learning goal will rarely be successful.
- Not setting a task for the duration of the narration of the story may lead to some learners becoming more disengaged.
- The length of the story needs to be long enough to serve the learning goal but not so long that learners become disengaged.
- The tutor must not be defensive if the group raises puzzles or questions that he had not foreseen himself. Rather this can be an opportunity for the tutor to praise the groups, or individuals concerned, for their sharp insights. In addition, the tutor can use this opportunity to raise awareness of the power of gathering different perceptions and the value of such open-mindedness to different viewpoints.

In the example of the foundry visit above, the tutor narrated the case study. In many cases, however, tutors will be required to provide written case studies. The checklist below highlights the main factors of a written creative case study.

1 Provide a strong narrative that draws the reader in and connects with the reader's experience. Be learner-centred in the choice of narrative.
2 A narrative that shows different perspectives, i.e. the young person, a member of an organization, an official, parent/carer – that is, 'characters' who share the experience but may see it from different viewpoints.
3 Lively and interesting writing that is short and to the point.
4 Provide a name for the case study that draws the reader in (though remember not to include ageing rock stars!).
5 The writing needs to have powerful sections that can be lifted and explored by groups or individuals; do not over-dramatize but

  have opinions, positions, strong ideas that learners can consider
  and discuss.
6   A sharp pace, avoiding unnecessarily long sentences or para-
  graphs; the Lifelong Learning Sector has readers of all standards.
  Consider the ability level of your learners and select accordingly.
  If the writing is too dense, the learners may switch off and become
  disengaged from the activity.

Having analysed the case study approach it is clear that the engagement,
developmental, and fun criteria for creative approaches hold true. Drawing
in the reader/listener by appealing to their interests, generating questions
and ideas by offering challenging perspectives that develop the learner,
while offering opportunities for engagement with their emotional as well
as cognitive selves, are the hallmarks of a successful case study. Case studies
do not have to be a dry, soulless tool that has been recycled lesson after
lesson. Used well, creative case studies can be an effective approach to
stimulating learning in the Lifelong Learning Sector.

So far in this part of the book, we have sought to offer creative approaches that focus on activities that can be used while the learning session is in progress. Some learners will warm to such creativity and be
active. Not all LLS contexts are so vibrant, however, and learners may
need greater stimulation. For the creative flames to burn, there needs to
be an ignition, a spark that sends the right messages to learners: 'this is
your space and what can be achieved here is inestimable'.

8   Creative Beginnings and Endings

This chapter focuses on how to fan the spark (discussed in the previous chapter) to prepare the learner for the task ahead and, moreover, to make them aware that learning is not theirs alone. By engaging in group activity, learners can achieve far more than by themselves or by passively staring at the tutor. This is not our total concern, however. Learning from peers in a group setting is about both give and take. Giving, in terms of feedback, energy, and pieces of themselves, knowledge and motivation. Taking, in respect of peer contributions promoting individual learning. Such processes need to be recognized. Too often groups achieve a great deal without any time given over to acknowledging the contributions of others to individual and collective success.

Creative teaching is about flow: how the tutor enables the learning space to have varying patterns of activity together with changes in pace. Surprise is a powerful tool to keep learners interested and captivated by what may come next. If their learning week, or day release from a workplace, comprises the same old activities, hour after hour, room after room, it is unsurprising that many start to feel disconnected from learning. Activities are important, but it is the transition between activities and sessions that is central to good practice. If done well, the learner is able to see how one learning experience builds upon another. Done badly, the session will be disjointed and the capacity for learning restricted. The learner possibly enjoys each respective activity, but fails to spot how the total session fits together or what learning has been gained. Therefore, the tutor needs to develop the skills to enable the transition from initial contact to further activity, so the session flows and builds.

The following two creative activities demonstrate a creative beginning and ending. The first activity focuses on the learner's initial contact with a new group, the transition into forming a sub-group, and the solidification of the sub-group identity. The second activity seeks to demonstrate how a group can recognize the contributions of individual members, as well as the cessation of the group's endeavours. After the activity has been described, the benefits and drawbacks of using this creative approach are highlighted.

A creative beginning: Lollipop Sticks to Centrepiece Activity

A new group is about to start a programme of learning. The tutor is aware that some learners already know each other since they are co-workers in the same organization. One of the aims of this programme is to ensure that learners are able to share experience from different settings. Consequently, the tutor needs to ensure that sub-groups contain learners from different establishments, as far as possible. This situation is common in the Lifelong Learning Sector, where it is important that learners mix with others in the group to ensure that they gain varied experiences and are made aware of, and challenged by, alternative perspectives. This important issue is also addressed in Chapter 9, 'Designing a Creative Session' (p. 93).

The obvious drawback with this activity is that learners are immediately taken out of their comfort zone. It is natural in a new setting and group for participants to position themselves alongside people they know, as opposed to deliberately sitting next to a stranger. More aware learners, however, may choose to do just this to fulfil a need for stretch and new experiences. In most cases, it is the tutor who encourages movement through the activity. To take learners out of this comfort zone, it is important to be clear on the reasons for this, and to contemplate how it is going to be skilfully carried out. Groups need to be enabled to form step by step, with a range of creative activities, building group members' confidence in being able to work and learn together.

The following activity identifies two key steps in creatively forming a sub-group, and then beginning the process of group identity. The activities are detailed in two parts:

- The first concerns the process of a new group meeting for the first time and then being split into designated sub-groups using lollipop sticks.
- The second enables sub-groups to begin to form an identity, a sense of belonging, and start the process of working together.

The forming of the sub-group and getting to know one another

1   Each new member of the group is issued with a lollipop stick. On one side they write their name. On the other side they write down an interest, or something that the others will probably not know about them (the content of which is of low risk as it is to be shared).
2   All the sticks are then placed into a bag, which the tutor shakes to ensure they are well mixed up.

3   Out of a group of thirty learners, the tutor may wish to form five sub-groups of six learners each. One member of the whole group is asked to take a stick out of the bag. They read the name out and that learner joins them and is given their stick. As they do this they pick another stick and that person joins them, who then takes another stick, and so on until all six sub-group members have been chosen. The sixth person picks the stick for the first member of the second sub-group, and the process is repeated until all sticks have been picked from the bag and the learners are in their sub-groups.

4   Once in their sub-groups, each group member introduces themselves by name. One member of the sub-group then holds all the sticks of that group, including their own, in their hand making sure that both sides cannot been seen. One member then chooses a stick (replaces it if it is their own) and reads out the interest/what is not known; the others are then invited to try and guess whom this refers to in the group. Once the group has guessed the member, the learner contributes something about the interest or fact.

Forming the group centrepiece

5   This next part of the activity is designed to start the process of building a sense of group identity. The sub-group is invited to place all their lollipop sticks in the centre of the table. The tutor also supplies some modelling clay (or equivalent) and drinking straws.

6   The tutor asks the sub-group to build a model, using all of their sticks and other materials, that symbolizes the group name they will give themselves. In addition, they are to design a logo that represents that name. A sticky label is supplied so the group can design the image of their logo.

7   The completed model, with its logo attached, is used to from the 'centrepiece' on the table in front of the group, where it remains while the six work together (see Figure 8.1).

8   Each sub-group is then invited to share their thoughts with the whole group about their chosen centrepiece.

9   From this point, the sub-group is referred to by their chosen name by the tutor and the other sub-groups of learners.

The benefits

- Moving from initial lollipop stick selection to group centrepiece is a step-by-step process that guides learners.

Figure 8.1   An example of a group's centrepiece (minus its logo)

- The random choice of stick by different members emphasizes fairness and transparency in the selection process and formation of sub-groups.
- The stick provides a vehicle for learners to share a small amount of information about themselves with others in a small-group setting.
- All learners are involved in the selection process.
- Choosing the name for the group is based on the use of a variety of creative tools, including model-building and graphic design for the logo. Creative thinking and hands-on craft activity are employed to create the centrepiece.
- Each person is represented in the centrepiece by using the six sticks to form its structure, thus reinforcing the message of belonging to a group.
- The centrepiece is a constant reminder to learners of the visual representation of the group and its initiation.
- Learners are involved in a range of tasks using different creative skills. This gives the tutor an opportunity to assess the variety of skills and talents that are being manifested early on in the programme.
- For large groups, the formation of sub-groups and their identity helps learners interact and be engaged from the start of their programme.

The drawbacks

- If the group is large, the selection process using the lollipop sticks as described above could be drawn out. Learners may become restless waiting for their turn. Therefore, the tutor needs to assess if this activity is going to fit the size and composition of the group.
- When first meeting with members of the sub-group, less confident learners may resist sharing personal information.

- Watchful facilitation is needed at this stage to ensure ground rules are observed, and some learners do not dominate or ridicule their peers' contributions.
- Part I of the activity is designed for a group who do not know each other. It is unsuitable for groups who have already worked together.
- If learners have been used to a constant diet of didactic teaching, and the tutor then asks them to be creative in both thinking and action, there may be some initial resistance.
- In the Lifelong Learning Sector, not all establishments have ready access to creative materials for the construction of the centrepiece.
- The aim of using the centrepiece is to reinforce group identity by locating it in the sub-group's workspace. At the end of the session, it will need to be stored and then retrieved when the sub-group re-assembles. Consequently, the structure needs to be robust enough to cope with this movement during and after sessions, as well as be stored securely. Ideally, the sub-group should take responsibility for their own creation, but this may not always be practical.

So the above has focused on a creative beginning to group activities using a variety of materials and techniques. Attention has been focused on a step-by-step approach to establish the group identity. The formation of a group is critical, but how group members end their work together is also significant. The next section of this chapter focuses on creative endings to group work.

The Farewell Gift Activity

(Taken from Eastwood et al. 2009: 29)

At the beginning of this chapter, we stressed that if learners recognize the contributions of others to their individual development, this will foster effective group learning. If a tutor is able to design and nurture a creative learning space where individuals support and challenge others, the expectation that knowledge and learning are going to derive purely from tutor input is dispelled. Recognition and acknowledgement of others' contributions is important. For those receiving the feedback, it fosters a sense of belonging and worth. The initiator of the acknowledgement also benefits from recognizing that engaging with and assisting others has enriched their experience.

 Again, in relation to employability, learners are accruing valuable skills. Modern workplaces often demand that employees become self-reliant. The removal of layers of management places heavy demands on individuals to self-manage, to seek support when needed, and work collaboratively with peers. Acknowledging such actions helps to oil the wheels of collaboration and breaks down the sense of isolation that can result from these environments.

The aim of the following activity is to enhance the learner's awareness of the contribution of others to their development. For some, leaving the learning space where they have gained so much can be difficult. Close working relationships have been formed and a great deal of learning achieved through working together. So the activity uses a creative technique to surface such feelings and leave the recipients with a physical 'gift' to take away from the learning space. Eastwood et al. (2009: 29) comment that 'this activity gives all learners a "feel good" factor at the end of the session and some positive thoughts to take away with them'.

1   The tutor explains to the whole group the importance of recognizing others' contributions to individual development.
2   Each learner is then issued with a piece of A5 paper, the stiffer the better (card is ideal but could be too costly for some LLS settings).
3   The learners form pairs with another they have worked closely with. Therefore, in a group of six there would be three pairs of learners.

Each learner is to consider their partner and complete the following three statements:
- 'Thank you for . . .'
- 'Something I would now like you to do is . . .'
- 'I appreciate your . . .'

The three statements are designed to encourage an appreciation of learning experiences as being reciprocal. First, an opportunity to thank the other person for what they gave their partner; second, the encouragement to go forward and act on something the partner has recognized or needs to be addressed; third, a recognition of a quality or skill that their partner has appreciated while working together.

It is okay if the learners wish to use an image instead of words on their card. They should be encouraged to make the card as attractive as possible; after all, it is a gift. For example, one member of a pair used origami to create a bird that for them symbolized their partner. On the body and each wing was the response to the three questions for their partner. Another chose to make a bookmark that separated out the three responses, so their partner could be reminded of these thoughts on a day-to-day basis. After working creatively together, it is amazing how inventive some of these farewell gifts can be.

4   The pairs then exchange their gifts. This can be done by the sub-group as a whole at the same time or on a pair-by-pair basis.

The benefits

- Learners like being given the opportunity to be involved with others at the end of a programme, especially when the experience has been a rich one (see below for the opposite scenario of an unpleasant experience).
- The exchange of gifts shifts the emphasis from the tutor's contributions to what the learners themselves have been doing, as active learners, for the benefit of others. Here the learning is owned by everyone involved, not just the tutor.
- Although this is the end of the programme, the exchange of gifts emphasizes that the learners need to continue to develop after they have finished working with their peers and the tutor. Learning is not to stop once they have departed from each other. This reinforces the key point that the person ultimately responsible for learning is the learner him or herself.

The drawbacks

- Problems can arise if the learner's experience in the sub-group has not been a good one. They may view this activity as an opportunity to get back at their peers by placing hurtful or spiteful comments on the gift. The tutor needs to reinforce the ground rules of the group to ensure that learners recognize they have a responsibility to others and themselves in the group. A skilled tutor will have accumulated knowledge of the potential 'problem pairings' in the group. By this point in the programme, the tutor needs to be ready to intervene and coach learners, so constructive feedback is given.

- In addition, the tutor may have to impress on the group that not all learning experiences can be programmed to satisfy every learner. Some experiences will be less enjoyable. However, it is important to stress that these can be still rich experiences if the right attitude is taken towards them: to consider what has been learnt, how it might be different next time, what the learner would be doing or would expect from others.

- If the group has limited feedback skills, constructing a balanced view of partners may prove challenging for some. The tutor will need to ensure that learners are prepared for the exercise. If giving and receiving feedback has not been part of the programme, this is an opportunity to develop the skills for learners (the following chapter offers guidance on a creative approach to teaching this important set of skills).

- Some learners may not consider such feedback of great relevance and believe only the tutor's comments have any worth. The tutor, through the design and facilitation of the programme, needs to have stressed the importance of learners interacting and formatively assessing each other's performance, wherever possible. If so, then the Farewell Gift Activity will be the final act in this vein. Otherwise, learners could feel self-conscious and awkward working in this way.

- Learners may be reluctant to share their views on others in this form for fear of being ridiculed, or just finding it hard to express such personal thoughts. The tutor may wish to discuss and then agree a ground rule that comments made on the gifts are shared between the pairs only. In this way, learners will be secure in the knowledge that their thoughts are not going to be broadcast to others outside of the pair. Again, if the tutor has engendered trust between learners, this shouldn't be an issue. However, groups differ, and individuals may alter their positions regarding others as the programme develops. As with all the activities described here, it is the tutor's choice, based on his or her knowledge of the group, to decide to run with an activity or not.

- Learners may be keen to design a gift for the tutor as well. The latter will have to impress on the group that the main aim of this task is for the learners to exchange gifts with each other. However, if that part of the task has been completed satisfactorily, then it is useful for the tutor to receive feedback, and to be seen as a learner in his or her own right. The group may offer some valuable developmental points in this form.

In conclusion, this chapter has explored the use of creative approaches to establishing a group and then ending the group. Throughout, the need for a step-by-step approach, which helps the session to flow, has been emphasized. Tutors can use creative approaches to engage and build confidence, as well as to encourage learners to be creative in establishing group identity, and recognize their own role and the contributions of their peers, in promoting individual learning.

The activities described above require the creative tutor to be aware of group process:

- How is the group progressing, in terms of both quality and quantity of interactions?
- If sub-groups are operating effectively, are individual learners enabling learning, and benefiting from group membership?
- Are sub-groups generating ideas and testing out new thoughts and actions?

In summary, learners need to be energized and engaged in learning. The tutor's work will be aided at this point by what has gone before. If ground rules have been established, re-addressed when necessary, and are jointly owned by learners and tutor, many of the potential drawbacks can be diluted or dealt with. The activities are a vivid illustration of how creative approaches to learning often need a transparent framework that learners operate within. The ground rules, together with the tutor's skilful group facilitation, are key components of such a learning framework.

9   Designing a Creative Session

In this chapter, we focus on designing a session to help enable successful creative practice. The emphasis here is on the practical: assisting the creative tutor to design a successful learning session. The creative teaching cycle (see below) will be used as a framework to identify the different components of the session. In addition, the needs of diverse LLS learners will be taken into consideration. Throughout the chapter, different creative teaching and learning methods will be proposed and reviewed for their practicality and effectiveness.

Figure 9.1 outlines the components of the creative teaching cycle, which consist of:

- The characteristics of the learners in the Lifelong Learning Sector
- How a creative session might begin
- Different creative teaching methods and resources to be used throughout a session
- Creative methods to recap and end a session
- Formative assessment and feedback.

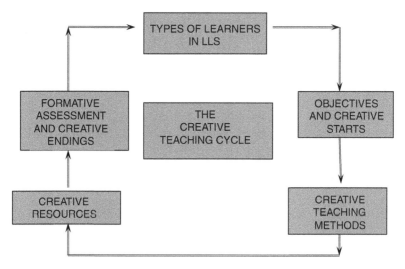

Figure 9.1 The creative teaching cycle

Types of learners in the Lifelong Learning Sector

As mentioned in the Introduction, LLS learners can be taught in a wide range of settings, including further and higher education, work-based learning, adult and community settings. The types of providers include school sixth forms, sixth-form colleges, further education (FE) colleges, universities, adult education services, prisons, private training providers, and in-house company training.

This wide range of settings emphasizes the diverse range of learners in the Lifelong Learning Sector and the different characteristics and needs they have. Normally, they are over 16 years of age and studying in post-compulsory education (although vocational courses are provided in some FE colleges and schools for 14- to 16-year-olds). Whatever the setting, a group of LLS learners, whether they be full-time or part-time, can vary widely in age, ability, and background.

Such diversity presents a number of challenges for the LLS tutor:

- How can this diversity be embraced?
- How can the session be inclusive so that all learners feel involved and take part?
- How can the tutor design the session to deal with the different learning abilities of the group, whereby both able and less able learners can be catered for?

Thinking points

Consider the diversity of the learners you work with in your practice. When you think about a session, how do you take their potential diverse needs into account?

In this chapter, we suggest a range of creative approaches and techniques to help address these issues and provide some useful guidelines for tutors. A session does not have to be crammed with 'all singing, all dancing' creative activities to make it successful. The ideas suggested here will offer opportunities to enhance the learning and engagement within the session and add variety for the learners.

Biggs (2003: 102) says a change in activity 'leads to a restoration of performance almost to the original level'. He also states that 'sustained and unchanging low-level activity lowers concentration'. An example would be attending a lecture, where the attention span of learners can be maintained for about 10–15 minutes before 'learning drops off rapidly'. Using different creative activities can help to address this problem.

At this stage, it is important to point out that planning creative teaching and learning sessions should not be confined to the younger or less able learners in the Lifelong Learning Sector. Time and time again, we have been told that 'these creative approaches won't work in my sessions, I teach adults. This type of thing is too childish'. Why should boring, conventional PowerPoint lectures be inflicted on learners just because they are older? Adults have a wealth of knowledge and experience to offer a group. By using a creative student-centred approach and collaborative working, these learners can bring a whole new dimension to the learning space. They thrive on new and exciting ways to approach their learning. Why shut them down through being passive participants?

Objectives and creative starts

Many texts discuss session objectives and what is required. Here, however, we focus on the objectives of a *creative* session. Over time, a tutor will assemble a range of activities to use with a group – a creative kit bag. But before dipping into this kit bag, the tutor needs to consider the group they are working with and the creative learning space.

To design and plan a successful session, the tutor must consider:

1   *The type of group.* The age, ability, background, and special needs of learners must form part of the planning. Consideration of inclusivity, diversity, and differentiation is vital. The same session taught to a different group of learners can often affect its success if these are not addressed.
2   *The learning needed to be achieved at this time.* If the topic is new, engaging and inspiring the learners' imagination and interest should be part of the objectives. When reinforcing existing learning, recapping and revising topics, more creative student-centred assessment approaches could be included in the planning.
3   *The length of session and time of day.* This is an important factor for sequencing and timing activities. Different approaches are often needed on a Friday afternoon compared with a Monday morning! Also a one-hour session should be organized differently from a three-hour session.

4   *The room and resources*. These can impact greatly on the creative session. Whether a computer room with fixed furniture, or a meeting room with no computer facilities at all, careful planning is required to include a range of activities. Similarly, a lack of materials may need some creative adaptation!

5   *The size of the group.* A large cohort of learners presents different challenges for the creative tutor. Inclusive student-active tasks can still be incorporated into the session, however. This is addressed later in the chapter, on page 111.

Often the creative tutor has to adapt the activities during the session to cope with these and other factors to maximize engagement and interest. Thus, deciding on the objectives of a creative session is:

> *a process of marrying the needs of the group at any one time with the potential range of activities contained in the tutor's creative kit bag.*

Through experience, the creative tutor recognizes that old activities can be adapted and shaped to accommodate the learning needs of a group. This contradicts the often-held perception that the tutor needs to spend many hours developing and designing creative activities. The key to efficient working is to reflect and consider how existing activities can be tailored for a particular group. Often learners can prepare the resources themselves, rather than the tutor do it. For example, in the dice activity on page 94, the learners can prepare the dice in the session and the accompanying questions to go with them.

Didactic, tutor-led teaching also involves considerable preparation time, although some tutors justify the time invested, claiming that student learning is maximized (even though they are passive participants). One of the key points in this book is that learning is not achieved in this way. Petty (2009: 141) supports this view, commenting that:

> many teachers develop one or two teaching methods and stick to them. This is a mistake. A variety of methods – as well as increasing student attention and interest – gives you the flexibility to deal with the wide range of challenging and infuriating problems that teachers inevitably encounter.

There are two distinct phases to setting objectives and creative starts. These are: the considerations to be made before the session begins and those once the creative session has begun.

Before the session begins

Before the session starts, there are ways to make an impact with your learners and help them focus. Creating the right atmosphere from the start is important. As we have already emphasized in Chapter 5, 'Classroom Management and Creativity' (p. 49), the layout of the room is the tutor's first consideration. It is not always possible to rearrange tables and chairs, but wherever possible, try and organize your room so that the activities you have planned can run effectively. It may be a case of just moving chairs within the session if tables are fixed.

Once the room is ready, consider having creative activities for the learners as they arrive. Learners can drift into the session over a ten-minute period, for a variety of reasons (their bus is late, previous sessions have not finished on time, etc.). This can result in a ragged start to the lesson, so having creative activities prepared to keep the prompt learners engaged and motivated is important.

Many creative tutors use *music* to enhance teaching and promote learning throughout a session. Before learners arrive, 'background music can create a pleasant and inviting learning environment and can be part of a strategy to welcome learners to a class. It can help learners to feel at ease, reduce anxiety and break down barriers' (Eastwood et al., 2009: 84).

Choosing the right type of music needs some thought. A learner might be allowed to choose the music, perhaps as a 'prize' for previous good work or behaviour. Sometimes a tutor may compile a 'playlist' of tracks relating to the topic of the session, and learners have to guess the connection. In Chapter 6, 'The Hooks of Engagement' (p. 57), we discuss how to 'hook' learners with music.

Duckett and Tatarkowski (2005: 43) discuss the use of Alpha music, such as popular chill-out albums, or baroque music at the start of a session to calm learners and mentally prepare them for academic work. We believe this can be particularly effective if the tutor is faced with a particularly lively group.

Pictures can also be used as part of a creative activity. A PowerPoint slide full of photos and images can serve two purposes: a link to a previous lesson, as a recap activity, or as an introduction to the new session. Additionally, these images could form a quiz for the 'early arrivers'. One colleague had a 'league table' on the wall, whereby the learners were continually given points for these types of activities, and the learner who came top at the end of the module won a prize.

Crosswords and word-searches have been used effectively to engage learners as they arrive, or as a recap exercise at the end of a session. These can be good to review previous learning or to introduce new terminology. Various websites provide free software for such activities, such as 'Hot Potatoes' (http://hotpot.uvic.ca/). Word-searches do not necessarily create any learning on their own, but they can be a fun way to introduce new terminology, which learners will then need to find out about, or have to explain words or concepts from previous learning. They can also make revision and recapping topics fun too.

Quizzes can be another fun activity. Questions on a PowerPoint slide or a gapped handout can keep learners engaged before the session starts. Again, these can be a useful recap exercise from a previous session or can assess existing knowledge of a new topic to be introduced. Learners could also do these types of activities in pairs or small groups. This can be especially useful when some learners have missed the previous session, as their peers can help them 'catch up' with missed information through the quiz activity.

Once the session has begun

The above activities are ways to create interest and link the session to previous ones. They can provide an impact in the lesson using pictures, music or questions, in a fun and engaging way. From the start, the aims and objectives for the session should be clearly outlined to put it into context and link the activities to date. Starter activities provide a good vehicle for questions and answers, testing prior learning and existing knowledge.

The following tips should help involve everyone at this point in the session and recognize diversity. Where possible, use nominated questioning (i.e. ask a learner by name) to encourage everyone to take part, otherwise there is a tendency for the more engaged or vociferous individuals to take over. Also, it keeps all of the learners alert. Having the learners' names on lollipop sticks is another fun way to do this. The tutor can draw a lollipop stick at random from a pot and ask that learner a question – this way no one is missed.

Questions can be adjusted to suit the ability of the learners to help promote confidence and inclusion. It is better to direct the simpler questions to the slower learners to build their confidence and contribution, and present the more able learners with the more challenging ones.

If the group is new to the tutor, or just a 'one-off' session, then the nominated-questioning approach won't be so easy and some simple icebreakers, warm-ups or 'name games' may be required at the very start. *Icebreakers or warm-ups* are vital when meeting new groups. Creative activities may not work effectively if the group and the tutor are new to each other. Building up a rapport with the group is important to develop the relaxed, comfortable atmosphere in which creative activities can take place. The best way to start developing this relationship is through knowing each other's names. In a single session, learning names is not always easy, so a good way to do this is using name badges (sticky labels are good for this) or place cards on the desk in front of the learner. Also, allowing a few minutes for the learners to introduce themselves to each other in pairs or small groups is a simple icebreaker, breaking down barriers and encouraging discussion. We discuss the formation of the group in Chapter 8, 'Creative Beginnings and Endings' (p. 80).

Dice can add fun to questioning, and can make this starter activity much more inclusive and interactive. As Eastwood et al. (2009: 75) comment, dice 'can increase motivation, interest and concentration while also offering the opportunity to develop learners' social and interpersonal skills'. The dice can be made from a card template, or alternatively from foam rubber cubes. If the die is being thrown around the room, a lightweight cube is vital to prevent injury. As the die is thrown from person to person, questions on the sides, such as 'What do you already know about this topic?' and 'What do you think will be interesting about this session?', can generate discussion.

If sticky notes are attached to the sides of the die, then they can be removed and the questions can be changed for further discussion during the lesson, or for recap questions at the end. Learners can have fun making their own dice too, and devising questions for their peers. As a tutor, these dice are ideal to save as a resource for recapping the topic in future lessons, or for using with other groups. Dice make a versatile prop to any session, as well as being used more conventionally for board games. Examples of dice are shown in Figure 6.1 (p. 59).

Sticky notes are a simpler means to start a topic or discussion, but not quite so much fun as the dice. Sticky notes can be handed out individually, and learners asked a question about the topic which they must answer on the note. Similar responses can be clustered together by the learners on a clear wall space in the room. From this the tutor can identify existing knowledge and understanding of group members, and use it as a basis to start the session or link to previous learning. Using sticky notes in a scorecard activity is explained in detail in Chapter 7, 'Encouraging Constructive Thinking and Exploration of Ideas' (p. 65).

Poster recap activities can be used to get a session under way too. This can work well part way through a learning module to put the session into context, or near the end of the teaching input to revisit the learning to date. In groups, learners have to record as many key points about the topic as they can. They can be encouraged to do this as a mind-map or as a diagram using a range of coloured pens to aid understanding. These can be pinned up around the room, with each group feeding back their contributions. This can be a good way to help bring previously absent learners up to date, and also for the teacher to assess learning among group members. Some tutors award points to the groups depending on the amount of information they have recalled. This activity can work well with a group of mixed ability, as the less able learners can have their learning reinforced by revisiting the topics, while the more able learners gain the benefit of constructivist learning (Petty, 2009: 7) as they make sense of their learning when explaining and 'peer tutoring' (Petty, 2009: 239) the others.

A *learning wall* can be used to help consolidate learning throughout the session and send positive messages to groups on how much they are achieving. The learning wall captures key terms, words, skills, and learning points from the beginning that can be revisited over the session. In effect, it is the 'learning story' for that group. Some tutors use a whiteboard to record key learning points throughout a session, but a large piece of flipchart paper pinned to the wall can be saved by the tutor at the end of a session and replaced and revisited next time. As the learning wall builds up with terminology and key words, the tutor can refer back to it to recap and reflect on what has been taught or used for revision purposes. Such devices should not be the mere preserve of the tutor. Learners can be encouraged to add their own significant learning to the wall. Such engagement can help less able learners, since such activity forms a constant visual reminder of their achievement throughout the life of the group. The tutor can then refer back to their posting at a later time to boost confidence.

Wherever possible, the tutor needs to look to enhance motivation and engagement and facilitate the learning process rather than thinking that they should be doing all the postings on the wall. The learning is the group's responsibility; the tutor is there to enable that learning.

Creative teaching methods

In the previous section, we explored session objectives and creative starts in the context of the tutor designing a creative session. Setting the scene and creating learners' interest in the session is important to generate the right atmosphere for creativity. We suggested some creative activities at the beginning of this chapter to help the tutor gauge learners' existing knowledge and to link the topic to prior learning.

In this section, we focus on the creative learning methods that can be used within the session. First, consider the typical characteristics that would make it creative.

Thinking points

If a colleague or a visitor walked into a creative session, what do you think they would observe? List some of the key words or phases to describe the events going on.

Here are some key words and phrases you may have identified:

- Students engaged
- Collaboration
- Challenging
- Problem-solving
- Colourful
- Different types of media
- Reflection

- Students active
- Student presentations/feedback
- Asking questions
- 'Hands-on' activities
- Fun
- Teacher facilitation
- A buzz

All of these characteristics would contribute to a creative session. The challenge becomes how the tutor can weave these into a coherent whole, so that learners progress through a number of creative phases to realize the session objectives.

In Chapter 7, 'Encouraging Constructive Thinking and Exploration of Ideas' (p. 63), we cover in depth the role of the tutor and group formation. In this chapter, the focus is on the practical; those creative activities that are in the tutor's kit bag to contribute to a creative session. As already mentioned, it is not about an 'all-singing, all-dancing' session, action-packed with one fun activity followed by another; it is about the sequencing of the activities so that there is a logic and meaning to the session. There has to be a purpose and a serious message behind the activities that encourages thinking, problem-solving, and learning. Little will have been achieved if the learners leave the session having had a great time but having learnt nothing, with the tutor following behind them exhausted and drained from all of his or her creative input.

The learning objectives for the session need to clearly outline the logical sequencing of each activity and how it relates to the overall outcomes. The timing for the activity needs to include a reflective space for feedback and an opportunity for linking the learning to the objectives. Such sequencing can be shared with learners at opportune times so that they can follow the various stages of the session as it progresses.

Good facilitation of creative activities by the tutor is often the key to their success. Here, we interpret facilitation as 'helping' the learners to explore concepts, to reflect on past and current understandings, and to check out and form new understanding with themselves, others, and the tutor. The learners' relationship to the course content is an 'active-reflective' construction, rather than a 'passive-compliant acceptance' (Light et al., 2009: 29). Usually, the tutor will have an opportunity to move around the room to listen and observe groups' progress. Individual learning can be prompted, questioned and challenged, and support given where necessary, especially with less confident learners. These are times when rapport can develop within the group. As this learner–tutor relationship grows, the trust and confidence between them will develop and, hopefully, encourage more creativity and learner interaction in the future. This relationship is explored in depth in Chapter 4, 'Introduction to Groups' (p. 39).

Often when facilitating a creative session, interesting and unplanned learning takes place, and valuable points and observations are made by learners based on their own experiences or knowledge. This is an ideal opportunity to praise and recognize learner contributions. Giving time to follow these up immediately and to share them with other group members can enhance the learning from the exercise. This impromptu feedback could take the form of the tutor inviting the learners to suggest what has been accomplished so far, discuss possible queries they may have, or highlight what may now unfold from this point on.

Facilitating a session effectively has two key effects:

1   It enhances the opportunity for flexibility of your session objectives. For example, an activity may be running very well and plenty of learning taking place. The tutor may choose to continue running with this and postpone a later activity.
2   It provides a fertile space for learner recognition. For example, tutors can take the opportunity to encourage learners to interact with each other, with the tutor, as well as engage in self-reflection. Didactic teaching allows little space for learners to critically reflect on their progress in this way.

A word of caution: because of the fluid nature of some creative activities, timing can be an issue. It is important to build in feedback and reflection, so setting strict time constraints on completing an activity can help, especially when learners have been asked to prepare something artistic or creative. Buzzers and whistles can make a fun end to activities, but music can make a good timer too. Some tutors play music for the final minutes of an activity, and then everyone stops when the music finishes. Duckett and Tatarkowski (2005: 43) suggest Beta music, which is prevalent in some pop music, is effective when tutors want their learners to be active.

The following are some methods that can be used in a creative learning session and that use the tutor's facilitation skills to full advantage.

A *learning carousel* of activities can be an effective way to keep learners engaged and motivated on a range of activities. By being constantly required to move around the room from one activity to another the learners stay active and participating (Eastwood et al., 2009: 42). Chapter 5, 'Classroom Management and Creativity' (p. 48), includes an example of a tutor using this approach and its positive effect on classroom management.

A *creativity café* is an excellent method for encouraging networking and sharing ideas within a session, especially when learners do not know each other beforehand. Eastwood et al. (2009: 21) advise that it 'encourages collaboration between them and the development of new approaches which everyone can chew through'. Harvey (2009) used this approach successfully with academic university tutors when sharing ideas around creative teaching.

Ground rules for the café have to be set from the start of the session:

- The room needs to be set out in a 'bistro' style (Figure 9.2). Using coloured tablecloths, flowers, 'Reserved for …' notices, and agenda 'menus' can add to the atmosphere (Figure 9.3). As well as tutors dressed as waiters!
- Learners have to sit at tables with others they do not know or do not normally work with.
- The learners share ideas around a given theme, prompted by a talk from a visiting speaker or a short input from the tutor.
- Comments are then recorded on flipchart paper and fed back by each table to the whole group.
- Learners mix again and move to a new table to discuss the next activity.
- At the end of the session, learners are encouraged to follow up afterwards at least one contact they have made.

Figure 9.2 Room layout for a creativity café

Figure 9.3 A creativity café table

This type of activity is an ideal way for different learners to share their own experiences and knowledge. By working with unfamiliar people, new and different perspectives around issues can be addressed and investigated. Often learners can have 'blinkered' views around a topic and until different alternatives are offered, these are not seen or recognized.

Simulation and case studies are discussed in Chapter 7, 'Encouraging Constructive Thinking and Exploration of Ideas' (p. 63), along with their benefits and drawbacks. These are excellent activities to encourage creative thinking, inclusivity, and differentiation within the group. Field trips and visits can provide 'first-hand' experiences for learners, though these are not always possible due to logistics, time, and costs.

Creative resources

In this section, we consider creative resources to be those items that support creative teaching methods. These resources are props – literally, these items 'prop' up the activity, enabling the learner to have a range of learning experiences that encompass their kinaesthetic, visual, and audio learning preferences.

Using props

Using props can enhance sessions in many ways. They can introduce a novelty factor to an activity, as well as provide a tactile element for kinaesthetic learners, for example. The following are some suggestions when planning a creative learning session.

In a Law class, **objects** were placed on the learners' tables. The learners had to identify how the objects related to the different law cases they were studying. The tutor found the learners recalled the details of the cases much more easily when they could make associations with the objects they had used.

In a Computer Studies session, a tutor placed a number of computer hardware components into a bag. Learners had to select an item at random and explain its purpose and function. This activity had greater impact than simply using pictures, because of its 'hands-on' perspective, which helps the more tactile, kinaesthetic learner (Petty, 2009: 149). A competitive element can be introduced into this type of activity, with teams scoring points for correct answers. This is also discussed in Chapter 6, 'The Hooks of Engagement' (p. 58), when discussing music and images.

The objects in the bag could be used for more abstract ideas and concepts. Learners can put items into a bag to represent a topic or theme such as 'Customer Service', and then have to justify their choice of objects to the group. This activity can be useful for reinforcing learning, embedding verbal language skills, and developing presentation skills. Eastwood et al. (2009: 16) also comment that 'the exercise promotes differentiation through task outcome and enables the teacher to assess knowledge and understanding'.

Hats and items of clothing are often used to enhance role-play activities. For example, hats can be used for distinguishing a leader, or jackets for business people. One tutor used forensic suits in a Law session to act out the detectives in a crime scene. The learners enjoyed the activity so much it was discussed by them for days afterwards. Normally, this was a session the tutor dreaded as the learners found the topic very dull. To add to the creativity of the session, learners can make their own props. In Chapter 7, 'Encouraging Constructive Thinking and Exploration of Ideas' (p. 69), for example, learners make glasses out of pipe cleaners in order to 'see' scenarios from different perspectives. This activity, with its benefits and drawbacks, is discussed in detail.

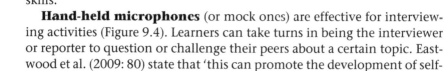

Toy telephones can be excellent props for customer service scenarios, or other similar communication activity. They help to develop and embed verbal communication skills, as well as enhancing learners' employability skills.

Hand-held microphones (or mock ones) are effective for interviewing activities (Figure 9.4). Learners can take turns in being the interviewer or reporter to question or challenge their peers about a certain topic. Eastwood et al. (2009: 80) state that 'this can promote the development of self-confidence and the use and application of appropriate communication

Figure 9.4 Using mock microphones for interviewing

skills in a variety of contexts'. Some tutors use them to control who speaks in the session, such as when organizing a debate activity, or for limiting the contribution of more talkative learners.

Random objects can be used in a session, such as tins of beans and soft toys, which have no obvious connection to the topic. Learners can be encouraged to use their thinking skills to make their own connections and meaning. For example, in a Business Studies class, tins of beans were used to discuss branding, and the soft toys for calculating product cost. Having the items on the tables added reality and focus to the activity, and again benefited the kinaestheitic learners who liked to hold the items being discussed.

Puppets can be a fun way to help interaction and communication, especially if the learners have to make them first. They can be used effectively with learners who are reluctant to contribute to a session. Often using a puppet as a vehicle 'to talk through' can offer a learner detachment from the topic being discussed. Eastwood et al. (2009: 69) note that they are good for 'dealing with sensitive and emotive subjects', such as workplace or parental conflicts.

Over time, the props that form in a tutor's kit bag start to accumulate. Also, once this form of learning becomes part of the tutor's practice, he or she will be cognisant of how everyday objects can be utilized for learning sessions. Charity shops, jumble sales, and 'pound shops' become rich hunting grounds for the creative tutor as he or she engages in planning for creative sessions with LLS learners.

The next section focuses on how creativity can be used for assessing learning during the session and for obtaining feedback from both tutor and learners.

Formative assessment and creative endings

During a creative session, formative assessment is a continuous process between learners and tutor, and is essential for the learning process. This is 'assessment for learning – it takes place during a course or programme of study, as an integral part of the learning process' (Avis et al., 2009: 170). Here, the focus is on designing creative recap activities to reinforce learning and assessing the effectiveness of the session by:

- Assessing the ongoing learning of the learner during the session (formative assessment).
- Generating feedback to the tutor on the learning that has been achieved, identifying gaps where further work is needed, and providing feedback on the level of engagement and enjoyment the learners derived from the session.

Formative assessment

Presentations are a popular way of assessing learning in a creative session. These can be formal, with PowerPoint slides and prompt cards, or less so, perhaps feeding back on a group mind-map or ideas-storming activity. They can be a valuable way for a tutor to assess learners' understanding and progress in a topic. If it is a group presentation, the tutor can also assess how well they have worked collaboratively. Offering different topics for the groups to present can add variety and interest to the session.

In today's world, building up learners' employability skills is very important. Encouraging learners to prepare and deliver presentations can build confidence and develop their communication skills, and often provides the opportunity for teamwork, independent study, and research. If learners are to cope with the fast-changing pace of society, then it is vital to encourage them, in a safe and comfortable environment, to develop the transferable skills they will need. Employers require employees to be good communicators, adaptable and flexible, able to problem-solve, as well as have the ability to 'think on their feet'. Simply memorizing facts and knowledge is not enough in our rapidly changing society. Simmons and Thompson (2008: 601) note that 'creative and cultural education is identified as having a key role in developing attitudes and skills required to prepare learners to take their place as flexible and adaptable employees and consumers in western capitalist societies'.

To build confidence in delivering presentations, providing praise and constructive feedback is essential. If learners are belittled or made to feel foolish in front of their peers, then trust will disappear and automatic negative thought processes will become entrenched (the ANTS of Chapter 3, 'Confidence and Creativity', p. 29). Petty (2009: 66) discusses the importance of 'medal and mission' feedback. To build confidence, it is important to give 'medals' and praise wherever possible and then offer 'missions' that are positive, supportive, and with constructive comments that learners can act upon.

Peer assessment can be used effectively in presentations, too, as it encourages listening skills, critical evaluation, and reflection. Using 'medal and mission forms' is a good way to do this. An example of a presentation form is shown in Figure 9.5. Giving the audience three 'medals' and one 'mission' when recording their comments encourages the learners to focus on positive and supportive aspects of the presentation, as opposed to the critical elements. Strict ground rules need to be set for giving constructive

PRESENTATION FEEDBACK	
To:	From:
Topic:	Date:
🎖️ MEDAL	
🎖️ MEDAL	
🎖️ MEDAL	
🎯 MISSION	

Figure 9.5 Example of a presentation form

and positive 'missions' to peers. Presentations should not be an opportunity for learners to pick fault with each other and undermine confidence.

When learners are preparing their presentations, encouraging them to use creative approaches will help engage and stimulate their audience.

Thinking points

PowerPoint does not always have to be used – learners can prepare posters, mind-maps or interactive presentations. Can you think of any other creative methods to be used in presentations?

One Law tutor used 'Come Crime With Me', adapted from the TV show 'Come Dine With Me'. The audience had to act as judges and feed back their comments, based on three categories: content, presentation skills, and creativity. This last category added a novelty factor to the session that the learners really enjoyed.

Figures 9.6 and 9.7 are examples of presentations prepared as posters. Figure 9.8 is an example of a recap activity where learners were required to prepare a poster on issues of classroom management without using text.

Figure 9.6 Example of a poster presentation

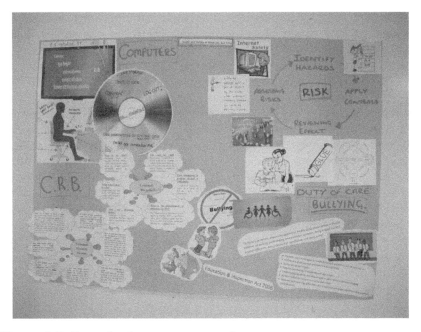

Figure 9.7   Example of a poster presentation

Figure 9.8   Example of a poster without text

Games can provide excellent creative recap activities for formative assessment. A wide variety of games are available to suit individuals, pairs, small groups, and whole classes.

Card-sorting activities are good for recapping and reinforcing learning. These can be matching cards or games such as dominoes, which can benefit the visual or kinaesthetic learner (Eastwood et al., 2009: 14). The concept is simple – a key word is written on one card, and this is matched to a definition. An example of a dominoes game is shown in Figure 9.9. The level of difficulty can be adjusted to suit the learners in question. The learners can prepare the cards themselves as a revision exercise, and test their peers. Cutting up a table of data to form a jigsaw is a novel way to test learners' understanding too.

Cards can also be used for ranking or classifying data. For example, identifying the recruitment and selection process in Human Resources, or a timeline in a History session. To add a fun element to this exercise, the cards can be hung as a 'washing line'. Figure 9.10 shows part of a 'washing line' identifying the timeline of changes in the English curriculum.

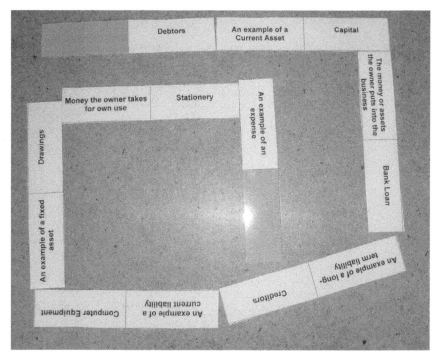

Figure 9.9 Example of a dominoes game

Figure 9.10 Example of a washing line

Board games, such as 'Snakes and Ladders', can help learners to recap topics. The players are only allowed to move around the board if questions are answered correctly. These games can be adapted to test higher-order thinking skills by having 'advice' or 'dilemma' question cards in the pack. These activities can be a good way to develop team spirit and competitive activities in the session.

Quizzes are always a fun way to recap on a session. They can bring a competitive element to learning and make good team games. Some websites provide free software for TV-style games, such as 'Blockbusters' and 'Who Wants to be a Millionaire?' Awarding prizes at the end can focus attention.

A dartboard with sponge-tipped darts (for safety!) can be another way to allocate points to a team. The team leader throws the dart and collects the points for the team if the question is answered correctly.

Bingo cards can provide a competitive and novel ending to a lesson. Ginnis (2005: 68) suggests each learner be given a blank 9-square grid that has to be filled in from a choice of twelve key words on the whiteboard. Learners cross out the key word on their card when the correct definition is pulled at random out of a bag and is read out. The first person to cross out all nine key words on their card shouts 'Bingo!' This can be a good way to reinforce unfamiliar terminology. Supplying the learners with marker pens and laminated cards that can be rubbed clean provides the tutor with reusable resources.

Mini whiteboards made from laminated white A4 sheets of paper can be an excellent resource. As well as having grids on one side for 'Bingo-style' games (or other useful templates, such as graphs or mind-maps), the blank side can be used by all the learners to write down answers to questions with a marker pen and hold them up at the same time. These can be used time and again for recap activities, since they can be wiped clean.

Generating feedback

Feedback at the end of the session is important for both tutor and learner. Generating feedback can help to ensure the tutor has achieved the learning objectives of the session. Before the learners leave the room, there are several ways the tutor can collect this information.

Using sticky notes is a simple way to do this. Each learner is given two different coloured sticky notes (or, alternatively, two different coloured pens). On one coloured note, they write down something they have learnt in the lesson, and on the other coloured note something they wish clarified further. The different coloured sticky notes are then clustered together on the wall, so that the tutor can identify any potential problems in their learning that can be addressed in the next (or a later) session.

A fun adaptation of this activity is building a hanging mobile. In groups, learners have to build a mobile using objects such as slide binders, pieces of dowelling, paper plates, string, rubber bands, and staples. Then they attach their sticky notes to their mobile. Each group then holds or pins up their mobile, and feeds back their learning and issues from the lesson.

(Taken from Eastwood et al. 2009: 91)

Mobiles can also be used throughout a session. For example, they can be used to attach sticky notes with new terminology and definitions, which can be a constant reminder to the learners in the session.

Postcards are a more confidential way for learners to provide feedback. Figure 9.11 shows a postcard one tutor prepared to obtain feedback from the session. The learners each completed a postcard and then posted it into a cardboard postbox. The feedback was helpful in two ways. First, it provided reassurance to the tutor about the content and activities used in the session. And second, it provided useful guidance and suggestions for the future.

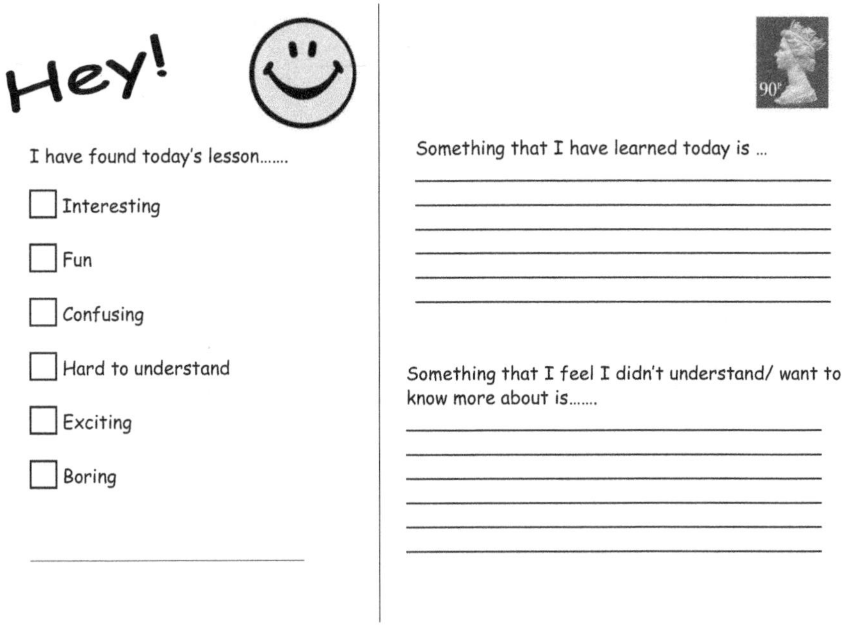

Hey! 🙂

I have found today's lesson.......

☐ Interesting

☐ Fun

☐ Confusing

☐ Hard to understand

☐ Exciting

☐ Boring

Something that I have learned today is …

_____

_____

_____

_____

_____

_____

Something that I feel I didn't understand/ want to know more about is.......

_____

_____

_____

_____

_____

Figure 9.11 Example of a feedback postcard (used with the permission of Laura Duxbury)

Modelling can be a powerful tool for learners to reflect on their learning. It gives visual and kinaesthetic learners an opportunity to 'talk through' their learning using objects and modelling materials, rather than completing rigidly written questionnaires. Using a model, learners have the chance 'to articulate and refine their ideas' (Eastwood et al., 2009: 18) as they explain different features of the model to their tutor and peers. Models can be used at different times throughout the learning process, and revisited at different times on the course. In Chapter 6, 'The Hooks of Engagement' (p. 58), we explore modelling as a way to use images in learning.

Models can be 'built' out of plastic toy bricks or objects, modelling clay or other materials, such as pipe cleaners, drinking straws, and matchsticks. They can be constructed into a structure, or take a more traditional form, such as a three-dimensional poster. See Figures 9.12 to 9.14 for examples.

Modelling has been used for activities such as reflecting on a learning journey throughout a qualification, and for understanding concepts such as 'Professionalism' on a teacher training course. Such methods can be used across a range of subject areas at all levels. Encouraging learners

Figure 9.12 Using modelling materials

to take photographs of their models provides a powerful reflective tool throughout their programme, which they can revisit.

Recording information by learners is a factor for tutors to be aware of. Collaborative work, such as mind-maps and posters, can result in individuals not having information for later recap or revision. It is important to encourage learners to take photographs of such resources, or to complete

Figure 9.13 Using toy bricks and objects

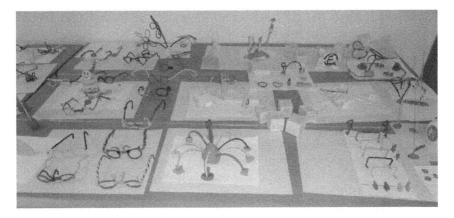

Figure 9.14 Examples of 'Learning Journey' models

written activities, such as a gapped handout after discussions or debates. If concepts are not captured by the learner in some way, excellent ideas and information can be lost when the session ends.

One of the common refrains of tutors when considering designing creative learning sessions is that they are inappropriate for large groups. The following seeks to address this concern, and offers suggestions on how tutors can still design a creative session with large numbers of learners. The emphasis is on boosting interaction between the tutor and learners, and among the learners themselves.

Creativity and large groups

Many tutors have to deal with large cohorts of learners in their groups, and often feel that creative activities are pointless for them, as they are impractical and unmanageable to execute in such settings. The following are ways to boost interaction when designing a creative learning session for large groups.

Thinking points

Consider how you could make the session with your large group more interactive.

The first example is *pairs/fours/sixes*. During a lecture-style session, learners are asked to discuss an issue with their partner. These two can then share their ideas with another pair or four learners close to them. Learners will be more confident sharing ideas with the whole room if they are generated in this way, rather than speaking as individuals.

Sticky notes can be distributed to the group to write down their answer to a question posed by the tutor. These can then be swapped around the room, so the learners selected to speak do not give their own answers. Alternatively, the notes can be gathered together at the front, and then notes selected at random by the tutor.

Throwing a foam ball around the room can be a fun way to respond to questions. If the person with the ball cannot answer, it is thrown to another person. This can be used for a team game too. The two sides of the room are divided down the middle, and if one learner cannot answer a question, the ball is thrown across to the other team. Points can be given to the teams for correct answers. The tutor needs to insist on strict ground rules regarding how forcefully the ball is thrown.

The tutor can also move around the room, inviting learners to raise or answer questions using a *roving microphone*. This time the microphone is used to interact with the tutor within the session, not as a prop for role-play as mentioned on page 100.

Using *mobile phones* is another way for learners to ask questions during a session. Some tutors use the computer to link the learners' phones to Internet sites, such as Twitter. During the session, the learners are able to post messages and questions for the tutor. To achieve this, the tutor sets up a discrete user account for the group, so only the participants in the session can take part. This can provide good feedback for the tutor when checking learning and understanding of the topic. Relevant or interesting comments raised by learners can be selected by the tutor within the session, and shared with them when appropriate. A note of caution, however: use of social media sites needs careful monitoring and ground rules to be established. It is recognized that not all LLS settings support such activities, whether as a part of policy or the lack of suitable technology.

Coloured cards can be a way to help interaction with the group. They can be used as True/False cards that the learners hold up. For example, a green card means 'True' and a red card means 'False'. Alternatively, green could mean 'I understand' and red could mean 'I am lost' – however, not all learners might want to admit this was the case!

Using *multimedia* can enhance these types of sessions. Backing up the topic with video clips, photos, images, and music can aid concentration and attention. In Chapter 6, 'The Hooks of Engagement' (p. 57), images and music were shown to be powerful tools to engage learners at the beginning and throughout sessions. Sudden noises or startling images add variety and aid concentration. Again, any additional media being used need to be assessed beforehand at this design stage for suitability for potentially diverse groups of learners. If the tutor is at all concerned that offence may be caused, then he or she should err on the side of caution.

Inviting learners to the front can add interest to a session. Learners could be required to take part in an experiment or demonstration, participate in role-play or deliver a presentation.

Although the above list is not comprehensive, it offers some help in increasing interaction with a large group. One of the issues to consider when encouraging interaction in such settings is the learners' confidence to speak out. As we mentioned earlier, working in pairs or small groups first can help to overcome this problem.

At this point we have reached the end of the 'creative teaching cycle', as depicted in Figure 9.1. There is the danger that if the tutor only uses a limited range of creative activities, the activities will lose their 'novel' impact and learners will become bored. What the tutor needs to avoid is learners commenting, 'Oh no, not another role-play!' or 'We did modelling last week'. When planning creative activities, the tutor needs to consider using a range of methods. The last part of this chapter features a tool to avoid such design faults by prompting the tutor to consider the full range of creative approaches that are available. This tool was developed out of the two-year TQEF project Creativity and Innovation in Teaching in Higher Education led by one of the authors at the School of Education and Professional Development, University of Huddersfield, UK.

Creativity tool: four categories of creative teaching

In this chapter, the planning of creative activities has been based around conventional teaching that most tutors experience on a daily basis, following the Creative Teaching Cycle, rather than using more radical approaches of working creatively with learners. In this final part of the chapter, we ask tutors to consider using the four broad categories of creative teaching identified in the Introduction (p. 3), as these will provide a varied session that embraces different aspects of creativity.

Four broad categories of creative teaching were identified in the TQEF research carried out by one of the authors (Harvey, 2009). These are:

1   The process of creative thinking
2   Creative teaching techniques
3   Creativity in community and employer engagement
4   Creative and innovative use of technology in teaching.

The *process of creative thinking* encourages learners to think 'outside the box'. Tutors use activities that encourage their learners to be critical, lateral thinkers. They are given problems and scenarios to analyse and evaluate.

Thinking points

Do you give your learners the opportunity to work ideas and problems out for themselves?
Are you doing all the thinking for them?
What creative activities can you incorporate into the session?

Creative teaching techniques help to make learning more fun and memorable for learners. These include such activities as games, modelling, and role-play.

Thinking points

Are your activities fun and engaging? Are they helping learning?
Are you giving yourself all the preparation work? Can the learners do this instead? Consider activities you could use.

Creativity in community and employer engagement brings real-life case study scenarios into the sessions through problem-based and work-based learning. This can include working with companies or organizations on marketing or sponsorship projects, or liaising with service users and supporting community-based initiatives. Working with employers and the community helps learners develop their employability and transferable skills for the future.

Thinking points

Do your learners see the relevance of their studies to the real world? Can they understand how the topic links to the wider picture outside the session?

Creative and innovative use of technology in teaching. Learners today use technology constantly, and some tutors try and embrace this in their sessions. Some use audio-visual technology, such as music, TV clips, and film. Learners can be encouraged to make their own film or podcast. Many tutors use computers with their groups, accessing Internet sites, virtual learning environments, and social networking sites. More than ever before, mobile phones are used for retrieving information, for voting and for texting data within sessions (see Chapter 6, 'The Hooks of Engagement', p. 61).

Thinking points

Learners today live in a world of computers, televisions, mobile phones and music. Consider how you are incorporating this technology into your sessions.

Figure 9.15 shows a Creativity Circle tool divided up into the four creativity categories. The Creativity Circle is a useful way to identify the

The 4 Broad Categories of Creativity in Teaching

The Process of Creative Thinking	Creative Teaching Techniques
Creativity in Community and Employer Engagement	Creativity and Information Technology

Figure 9.15 A Creativity Circle

categories of creative teaching methods used when designing a varied creative learning session. Large segments that are left blank may suggest an imbalance in the variation of activities offered in the creative session.

Thinking points

Colour each segment in the Creativity Circle to match the percentage of creativity you use in that particular category. How colourful is your circle? Can you identify any imbalances? List the types of activities you could offer in each category to fill any gaps.

Conclusion

In this chapter, we have focused on designing a creative learning session using a range of possible teaching methods and approaches. We have presented a variety of creative teaching activities that can be used in designing and planning a creative learning session. Using a wide range of activities is the best way to maintain a high level of learner motivation and engagement. It is also worth noting that if the same creative idea is used again and again, this can be as demotivating as a didactic teaching session. So, using activities that are distinctive and innovative will have the most impact. We cannot stress strongly enough the importance of the objectives of the session fitting the needs of the group, with the tutor's creative kit bag being dipped into for appropriate activities that will deliver the outcomes for the objectives. Preparing a creative space beforehand, which whets the learner's appetite, can generate a positive attitude for the 'main event'. Icebreakers, questioning, and activities to test prior learning and existing knowledge send a clear signal to learners that they are to be engaged by both you the tutor and their peers. By employing the four categories of creativity, as described by the Creativity Circle model, learning will never be the same again for your active and engaged learners!

Part 3

The Organizational Context

Just as with effective teaching, we think it important for you, the reader, to be clear on what we have covered so far, and what is coming next. In particular, how the first two parts of the book relate to this last part.

Parts 1 and 2 focused on the individual and group dimensions of creative approaches to teaching in the Lifelong Learning Sector. We have shown that the individual is a key component in ensuring that creativity is developed and fostered. There is a need for the individual practitioner to have a clear understanding of their capabilities and the confidence to enable creative approaches in a learning setting. Moreover, the three dimensions of creative space (the mental, the physical, and 'the space between') demonstrate that creativity is a dynamic process between tutor and learners, and learners and their peers.

In Part 2, 'The Group Perspective', we explored the impact of learning in groups on this dynamic process of creativity. Using examples from the authors' experience, the importance of classroom management and engagement of learners in a group setting was described. The tutor is a facilitator, an enabler of learning, encouraging the generation of ideas and exploration through engagement with others.

This final part of the text considers the third dimension of creative approaches – the Organizational Perspective. To this point, the tutor has been viewed as working within a bubble that contains themselves and their learners. The LLS settings described in the Introduction have not featured to a great extent. These particular learning contexts can, however, impinge on everyday practice. For example, a tutor may be working in a further education college that is being restructured or subject to a quality review, there may be resulting anxiety about jobs or future roles, team and line manager relationships may come under strain, and as a consequence, the workload increases. All these factors may affect the creative mental and physical space. Tutors may be less likely to adopt new methods for fear of failure, or may not have the energy to develop creative materials to use with their learners. An alternative scenario could be that a freelance tutor may be asked by a voluntary agency to help establish and then facilitate an action-learning group formed of staff and service users. The tutor is keen to use creative approaches with this new client, even though they have never worked with a voluntary agency before. The respective learning contexts of the further education college and the voluntary agency may be different in many respects – their strategy, types of learners, possible physical space, tutor support, and assessment of performance. What happens in the creative 'space between' will therefore be affected by the organizational context the tutor is working within.

Thinking points

Consider the organization(s) you work in. What are the characteristics of that organization(s), both positive and negative, that affect your work? E.g. people, resources, style of management, programmes, and types of learners.

Whether you are a practising tutor with many years of experience or a newly qualified practitioner keen to develop exciting and engaging ways of working in a new job setting, having an awareness of the organizational context is crucial. When one of the authors was on their initial teacher-training programme, they were given just one piece of advice relating to the organizational perspective: 'don't sit on someone's favourite chair in the staffroom'. A useful tip at the time, but greater organizational awareness is needed to develop creative approaches in practice. Consequently, Part 3 seeks to redress this imbalance. It is formed of two chapters.

Chapter 10, 'Stimulating Creative Change in Your Practice', explores bringing about creative change in practice by considering:

- ways of understanding the tutor's organization where they practise
- building and sharpening the idea that is to be developed
- methods of getting others involved, on-board, and supporting the change.

Chapter 11, 'Looking after the Creative Tutor', focuses on looking after the creative self. All of the above are worthless if the practitioner is not conscious of their own wellbeing and how this can be nourished. The chapter stresses that, for creative practitioners, this is even more relevant as they need to be regarded by themselves, and others, as jewels in the crown of the Lifelong Learning Sector: for they offer the means for engagement and retention of students, as well as the fuel for innovation and development of programmes. Without looking after themselves they cannot hope to meet the needs of the sector at this time, and in the future, let alone enjoy their lives outside the workplace. Chapter 11 thus highlights and offers advice on:

- why wellbeing is important for the creative tutor
- the potential fallout from the stresses and strains of the job
- the need to stay professional
- a focus on 'me'
- self-worth and self-talk
- five ways to wellbeing.

10 Stimulating Creative Change in Your Practice

This chapter seeks to help tutors who wish to initiate and develop the creative practices we have described in the text so far. They could be a new tutor in an LLS setting appointed to inject creative approaches into an existing team, or an established tutor seeking to refresh their own practice and bring other colleagues alongside them. Alternatively, the tutor may not have much choice. For instance, their particular learning setting may have been subject to a quality review and been advised to adopt different approaches to combat low attainment or attendance. In all cases, more focus is to be placed on developing creative approaches to learning.

So where do we start? A common refrain is that farmers do not grow crops; they provide the conditions that allow the crops to grow. Similarly, if tutors want to bring about a change in practice, they have to understand the learning context, in its widest sense. If they are aware of the conditions that will allow the creative seed to develop and then flourish, there is a greater chance of a bumper crop. A lack of awareness will more than likely result in a weakened initiative that withers and dies.

Do your research: ways to look at your practice

Learning settings are complex places. They involve power relationships: between tutors and learners, managers and tutors, senior managers and governing bodies. Internal and external politics are played out in learning settings, becoming intensified when resources become scarce, as particular subject areas and individuals jostle to protect their identity and survival. Any tutor wishing to bring about change needs to have a keen sense of such dynamics if that change is to be successful. Without an awareness of the factors that may help and hinder the change, the tutor will be committing a great deal of time and energy that may, ultimately, be wasted. Making sense of all of this remains a tough challenge for inexperienced (and many experienced) tutors. Therefore, it is critical that if a creative change is required, tutors do their research. The current situation they work in has to be unpacked and understood so that effective planning can take place.

A useful tool for understanding an organizational context is the following adaptation of McKinsey's 7-S Framework. In a seminal text, Peters and Waterman (1982) presented this tool as a way of diverting thinking away from seeing organizations as purely structural – made up of hierarchies, departments, and organization charts. Such a simplistic view failed to take into account the complex working of organizations. More important was the way in which the components of an organization – both 'soft' and 'hard' factors – were coordinated. Here we use these 7-S components to explore key organizational factors when introducing a creative approach to learning:

1   *Strategy*: What are we trying to achieve? Is the initiative clearly described? If a more sceptical colleague asked you what you were intending to do, could you succinctly explain it to them? Moreover, have you thought through how you are going to initiate this development?

2   *Systems*: What are the systems of work that the tutor needs to consider? These may be programmes the tutor has to follow, or the assessment processes that impinge on how and what is learnt.

3   *Structure*: How is work organized? In year groups, within a department, a faculty, an external controlling body, such as a central government department financing an initiative?

4   *Staff*: Who has influence in your immediate practice and wider network? Who might be most affected by this initiative? Who might be the biggest supporter/resistor?

5   *Skills*: Which skills will be needed to make this initiative work? Who else has skills that might be needed?

6   *Style*: How does change occur here in the practice setting? How are new innovations managed, or not? Can a former successful innovation be researched and learning transferred to this development?

7   *Shared values*: What is the passion here? What is important for the practitioner about ensuring this initiative is successful? Do others share that passion?

By using the above prompts, the tutor is able to assess which factors are most important in any given situation they wish to change. Moreover, the interplay between factors is crucial. For example, the relationship between structure, systems, and staff helps highlight how work is organized, what constraints may be imposed, and who could be a positive or negative influence on the planned change. This relationship is explored later in the chapter.

A further useful model is one that assesses the power and influence of relevant stakeholders. Both Bourne and Walker (2008) and Walker et al. (2008) stress the importance to all project managers of understanding the political landscape in which the change will take place. By visualizing this landscape through development of a model showing relative power and influence, stakeholders that have the potential to stimulate progress or stifle a new innovation at birth can readily be identified. Innovation is not purely a rational act. It involves emotions, and creative practitioners tend to have a drive and energy that others lack. On occasions this may be an advantage. Passion such as this is infectious, especially among learners who quickly attune themselves to a more exciting and engaging form of learning. It is necessary, however, as the challenges above suggest, that the developer recognizes other colleagues may not share the same passion. Colleagues may feel deskilled by what is being proposed, initially believe that a lot more work is required, or do not share the same view of the learner held by the creative practitioner. Consequently, introducing different ways of working will require a political nous, ensuring that supporters are mobilized and potential resistors acknowledged and engaged with. The following section outlines how the creative innovation can be designed to ensure maximum impact.

The Trojan Mouse

Unless the tutor is lucky to have vast financial support, most change will be initially small and focused. Thus, a particular group of learners or programme may be targeted for creative approaches. Alternatively, a group of tutors may decide to adopt a different way of working and support each other's professional development. There is a danger of running away with an idea, trying to be too ambitious with constructing materials or adopting an unrealistic time frame. Much will depend on the response to the 7-S checklist above. If the culture is dominated by didactic teaching, and has always been so, there will be a tough challenge ahead. The tutor might, however, be in a learning setting where senior managers and colleagues support innovation with visible action rather than mere rhetoric. Like any successful construction, thought needs to be given to its foundations. A well-designed, clearly thought-through development, which the tutor can demonstrate is an advance on current practice, will provide a solid foundation for subsequent development. This can be termed the 'Trojan Mouse'. Here we design a tough, thick-skinned development that, like all mice, is quick to breed!

To nurture the 'mouse', our resilient rodent of an idea, avoid potential traps by:

Determining the need

Thinking points

Clearly identify what needs to be changed and improved. Think carefully about the current situation and highlight what is happening now that tutors and learners need to address. Such issues might include poor attendance or retention, reluctance to get involved in learning sessions, poor results, learner feedback, lack of morale among tutors.

Shining the spotlight on you

Thinking points

If the tutor who is initiating the change is not passionate about it, they will find it hard to get others involved. Ask yourself: What is your passion here? What are you most excited about? What potential is there to bring about something different? If your responses are positive to all these questions, then proceed.

Visualizing

Thinking points

If the change went ahead, what would be in place that is not happening now? What would your learners be doing and feeling? How would you be acting and feeling? What would your learning space be like? Close your eyes and imagine that space – the sights, colours and sounds, how learners are interacting with you and their peers, the achievements they are making in their learning.

There is a tension that lies at the heart of creativity: between the space being different, expansive, experimental, with the taking of risks, while at the same time needing discipline, fortitude, focus, and a systematic step process. De Bono (1995: 72) describes this admirably, when he states: 'Information and logic set the framework. Creative design offers the possibilities. Information and logic assess the possibilities'.

Planning

Thinking points

Now consider formulating a plan. What would be the logical sequence of achievable events that will bring your idea to fruition? Yet there is another purpose: to convince and recruit others to our cause. A plan serves to engage with other potential followers. Who might they be? If a plan is presented that is logical, well considered and contains identifiable, desirable goals, we are more likely to support it than one that lacks these qualities. It gives the potential supporter the confidence that ambiguity, an inevitable change factor, can be worked with, within a process. So how could you make those goals desirable to others, so they want to be part of your plan?

Until now the discussion has focused on the individual tutor wishing to develop his or her practice. For example, in the above explanation of the Trojan Mouse, the advice is to persuade and bring on board others through the clarity and attractiveness of the plan. Much can be gained, however, from organizing alongside others to improve practice in collaboration.

Action research

Action research has real benefits for developing creative approaches to learning. Unlike traditional research, where the researcher stands apart from what they are researching, tests hypotheses, and seeks to apply generalized knowledge, action research is rooted in the particular context. Thus, creative practitioners are both the agents and the subjects of the research, using a critically reflexive stance to explore, alongside others, their particular practice context to bring about improvement and creative change. As McNiff and Whitehead (2009: 13) state: 'Action Research is about improving knowledge about existing situations, each of which is unique to the people in the situation, so the knowledge cannot be generalized and applied, although it can be shared'.

Moreover, action research is a collective approach to development, where individuals come together around a shared concern or inquiry. Stephen Kemmis has written extensively on action research and his work is useful here because it is rooted in changing educational settings. Kemmis and McTaggart (1988: 5) see action research as a *'collective self-reflective inquiry that is carried out by participants so to improve the rationality and justice of their own social or educational practices, as well as their understanding of these practices and the situations in which these practices are carried out'*. This perspective fits well with the Lifelong Learning Sector, since as practitioners we endeavour to engage and stimulate different approaches to learning for an increasingly diverse learner population. Such a purpose stresses that social and educational practices are linked, a clear rationale and dedication to a just practice for our learners. If tutors can collectively organize and inquire, usually in small groups, about their learning spaces, then improved understanding and practice can be achieved. An example of action research in practice is described on page 128.

This form of research has at its heart the 'critically reflective' approach to action research, especially the Critically Reflexive Action Research (CRAR) model proposed by Weil (1998) and others (Reason and Rowan, 1981; Lather, 1991; Reason, 1994). Here, learning is seen as engaging with contradictions and dilemmas, through reflection in, and on, action (see Figure 10.1).

The CRAR model highlights a series of steps:

1. *Starting problems/dilemmas.* Initially, we seek to raise awareness of the contradictions and dilemmas experienced by practitioners. These include starting assumptions of what tutors understand by 'creative practice' or improving the learning space. For example, the inquiry may focus on experiences where learning has been blocked, or is considered unsatisfactory, and needs a boost of creativity. In addition, the inquiry could explore some of the history of initiatives that have sought to develop such 'attitudes' or 'practices/competences' within other learning spaces – at a college or organization the participants are aware of, for example. It is important to focus on the participants' own constructions, how they view the current situation, so these can be captured and then played back to highlight the limitations and potential of existing understandings and processes.

2. *Focus and frame inquiry cycle in context.* The second step is to focus and frame the inquiry cycle while engaged in it, so facilitating both individuals and groups to plan and enact more insightful choices. The first step probably generated many different views and perspectives. For the inquiry to have some practical focus, it needs to have a subject of attention and energy. The group needs to identify what they share, which area of their

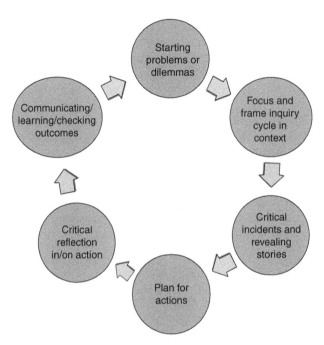

Figure 10.1 Critically Reflexive Action Research (CRAR) (adapted from Weil, 1998).

practice was the common theme in Step 1, and so what they choose to work on as a starting point from many possibilities.

3. *Critical incidents and revealing stories.* The third step leads to a deepening of understanding of the key questions of the inquiry. The inquiry may contain a number of revealing narratives where tutors relate critical incidents of frustration, despair, detachment, and disempowerment. The intent here is to explore and document these, and for group members to 'feed back' to the other participants their reactions and interpretations of what they have had heard.

4. *Plan for actions – individual, group, x-group, organizational.* Again, the intent is to enable the individuals and groups to put the conjunctions and disjunctions that have been brought to the surface into perspective. What different choices could be made in such circumstances? Say a desired action is to introduce more learner involvement and move away from a didactic style that clings to PowerPoint. What actions might be generated as a result? It could be that the group decides to share ideas on introducing more group work with a specific cohort of learners, or to use puzzles and models to stimulate learners 'individual reflection and questioning skills.

5. *Critical reflection in/on action.* Surrounding each of these is the 'cloak' of critical reflection. Thus, action, wherever present, is scrutinized and challenged in both self and others. Coghlan and Brannick (2005) see reflection as the glue, bonding research and action. Consideration of what the group was doing (the content), how they decided to go about it (the process), and what assumptions were present at these decision points (the premise), allows both individuals and the group to uncover their experience and work with it. Fresh actions then become rooted in an exploration of what has occurred, and how the action research group's learning can be built upon. We have to be respectful of the difficulty of changing behaviour in contexts where traditional learning approaches are entrenched. Identifying what actions seem purposeful and how potentially others (including the tutor carrying out the reflection) are helping and hindering the planned change is essential if development is to occur.

6. *Communicating/learning/checking outcomes.* The group evaluates what outcomes and learning have occurred and how these may be communicated to significant others. The latter may include external and internal stakeholders such as managers, peers, and learners. At this point, the group may decide to re-engage with the original inquiry cycle. For example, the outcomes may indicate that they made an incorrect judgement when introducing the creative change and they need to embark on a new cycle of inquiry. The example that follows illuminates such a process using a real case scenario in an LLS setting.

An example of CRAR in practice

	Stage of CRAR	What is happening?
1	Appreciating starting problems/dilemmas	Learners reluctant to get involved in discussions in class. Starting assumption is that learning is being held back by learners' behaviour. An action research group of five tutors gets together to decide what they can do about it
2	Focusing/framing inquiry cycle in context	Tutors look for books or other sources to help them with solutions. They decide to allow learners to work in pairs more often in their different learning spaces, the rationale being that learners will have the opportunity for peer discussion

3	Broadening/ deepening of inquiry	The action research group decides to focus their actions on Year 1 Business learners. They also recall similar stories of trying to do something like this before
4	Reframing/ refocusing inquiry	Reflections on previous experiences are taken into account and mistakes that were made are to be avoided. Two tutors have some reservations based on lack of experience. The others state they will support them with coaching and encourage them to be involved
5	Planning for insightful actions	Each action research tutor contributes to how and when they are going to initiate the pair work. The action research group agree on a time and place when they will meet to review the actions taken. They act
6	Critical reflection on actions	At the subsequent action research group meeting, the experiences are reflected upon. Those who were reserved about the planned changes remark how well it worked and how the coaching by the others was very helpful. More learner discussion resulted from the tutor actions. It was revealed how the pairs started to work with other pairs without prompting
7	Communicating/ learning/checking outcomes	The action research group decides to feed back to the learners their approval and inform senior management of the outcomes. The action research group discuss the need to change the layout of a room to facilitate better interaction. A room change is sought for that session to overcome this. The action research group has learnt that the original plan has worked, they can work together successfully by supporting and challenging each other, and also that they want now to press on and introduce more group work. They start to discuss what are the dilemmas around this ... and the cycle continues to a new Step 1.

The cyclical nature of the CRAR model is helpful as a guide for tutors, and other participants, to inquire into their practice. They then take these reflections of processes, knowledge, relationships, and issues back into the particular formal and informal encounters they have with learners as actions. So we have an ebb and flow of *considering – planning – action*. This is followed by consideration of those actions, further planning resulting from this research, with their consequent actions, and so the process continues in a series of cycles of inquiry. Often described in terms of evolving cycles that progress, such a view tends to overlook the fact that sometimes the momentum of change does not circulate in such a positive form. An ebb and flow is a better description because it depicts pauses and flows that are not always regular or purposeful. Sometimes the reflections are difficult to get grips with, or the actions do not result in the desired outcomes determined at the planning stage.

Nevertheless, action research is ultimately a *practical* process, rooted in everyday experience, which, when engaged in rigorously, leads participants into further cycles of inquiry. Reason (1999) makes a useful point when he states that the rational order of the above stages can be highly effective in the early stages of an inquiry group. Here, a structure and a sense of 'knowing what we are doing and where we are going' are needed. If creativity and experimentation are required, however, such a rational model is too rigid a structure. There needs to be a balance between systematic order and 'chaotic interaction' between members. The interconnections between the latter, and growing understanding that the group can tolerate imaginative diversions, unsettling challenges and divergent thinking, will enable new forms of thinking and working. The key lies in the group's ability to tolerate such potential chaos and ambiguity. As Reason (1999: 213) states: 'The key validity issue is to be prepared for it, to be able to tolerate it, to go with the confusion; not to let anxiety press for premature order, but to wait until there is a real sense of creative resolution'.

Coghlan and Brannick (2005) point out that such tolerance and inquisitiveness require being skilled in a collaborative approach. Unlike an external researcher looking in, the tutor is living this research; they are part of the inquiry. They will have thoughts and feelings based on their own experience that need to be shared, held up to the light and tested. Such ideas and opinions need to be illustrated with experiences, so others can then see how that standpoint has been arrived at, and whether it matches the perspectives they hold based on their own experiences.

Capturing reflections

Development work can sometimes be exciting and creative, but also confusing and chaotic. Engaging in development involves new ideas, experiences, and data to capture and make sense of, then planning for the next action – a heady mix. Busy, pressured work environments do not always lend themselves to reflection. Yet, as explained above, finding time and space for reflective activity is essential to link the research to the action. Amidst all the potential chaos there is a need for programmed calm. An often-heard objection is that such calm is in short supply in contemporary workplaces. Nevertheless, the engagement in these reflective activities is essential if tutors are to effect positive change. Committing time and energy is an investment. So it is important that tutors determine whether there is a return on that investment. Cotton (2011: 175) says that an underpinning philosophy of action research is that 'genuine sense of having time and space to understand the impact of actions on individual learners'. Finding time for reflection on informal and formal conversations with learners regarding how they are experiencing the creative approach can be informative. Moreover, it helps the tutor to focus finite energy on what works and understand what prevents other proposed actions. In the next chapter, we return to this subject in our discussion of the creative tutor's wellbeing; here the emphasis is on finding space to further the action research process. One's own process of reflection is a personal choice. Knowing what works is the key: it could be a warm soak in the bath, a walk with the dog, or a partner who is a good listener.

When working alongside others, the tutor may need to find a way of capturing collective reflections. A reflective diary is extremely useful as a joint record of what was being experienced, thoughts and feelings, learning, and planned actions. Who collates the diary? The task can be allocated to a member of the tutor group who is adept at picking up from the discussion the reflective elements. Or, to avoid the possible danger of relying on just one listening post, the role can be shared so a different member collates the diary each time the group meets.

The process of capturing reflections and the narrative of the inquiry does not necessarily have to be in physical form. The use of an electronic wiki, where members of the action research group have the opportunity to freely and spontaneously contribute ideas and perspectives, can act as a useful reflective tool. Similarly, a simple blog that includes visual material and written reflections serves as a helpful device that any member can contribute to at any time. Some vital reflections can occur at any time, day or night, so it is advantageous for the group to have this flexibility to enter useful data for themselves and others. In addition, encouraging learners to write about their learning experiences and what has worked for them, why, and how they intend to find opportunities to transfer the learning from these experiences, helps their own reflective process. As a consequence, the creative tutor can capture valuable data on the impact of different approaches they have employed in their practice (Harvey, 2007).

Throughout this chapter, we have sought to strengthen the case for creative change by investigating the context of the practice, constructing the Trojan Mouse, and involving others to combine research and action. As the final component of the CRAR model indicates, communicating the outcomes to others can convince doubters and boost further support. If only change were so simple. After all this, the creative practitioner may still experience resistance within their organization. The way forward is to maximize the message through creative methods of engagement, especially with those practitioners, and other stakeholders, beyond the immediate practice context.

Reaching out

> I refuse to intellectualize, or try to understand how it happens. It happens, and I just try to ride with it. And the frightening thing is when it doesn't happen, it's actually terrifying because you realize, 'I've dried up. It's finally happened: the well is empty.' But, then if you get through those periods, then something starts happening again. A lot of what happens, it's like doing a painting without actually doing a sketch in advance. You just start and you got this, you add another thing, boom, boom, boom.
>
> (Gilliam, 2012)

The above quote identifies the randomness of so much creative activity. Terry Gilliam, considered to be one of the most innovative filmmakers of his generation, refuses to intellectualize about inspiration; as he says, sometimes it happens, other times it 'dries up'. What he does is to try and 'ride with it'. As a creative practitioner this may sound very familiar. Nevertheless, we believe that there has to be a balance of 'going with it' and a strategic plan to realize the intention. What Gilliam does identify is the fortitude to accept difficult times and potentially the situation will change. The LLS, as we have discussed, is fraught with tidal shifts of policy and opinion. Many of these shifts are cycles of former ideas that come to the fore again. The emergence and re-emergence of initiatives helps to breed a cynicism that 'we have seen all this before' and apathy rules. Such contexts can be energy-sapping for the creative practitioner, leading to acceptance of the status quo, or a quick exit at the first opportunity.

However, if we have a clear intention to develop creative approaches, and there is evidence of these having a positive impact on learners, then others need to know. Such strategic spreading of the word has two effects. The first is that it bolsters the developer's case for the approaches being supported in their own workplace. Second, it provides succour to other practitioners who are facing the same difficulties but have the same creative intentions. Therefore, the internal shifts in attitudes and the connections made externally are linked. One can support the other.

Mosley (2011) provides some very useful pointers on how to raise the creative practitioner's internal profile:

- *Stand up and be counted.* Recognize that you have expertise as a creative practitioner who has identified a need, worked alongside colleagues and learners to make it happen, and have the humility to recognize that there is still a lot of learning to do.
- *Raise your profile.* Are there opportunities within your workplace(s) to demonstrate your skills and knowledge? Within the author's practice we have given talks to other staff, attended meetings and spoken at various internal meetings – team meetings, departmental gatherings, staff development seminars – to share our knowledge with others. We have also run creative workshops for colleagues, or presented at other workplace gatherings, as well as offering help to colleagues who are facing problems in changing their practice. In so doing, the creative practitioner is visible, is known, and develops the reputation for being the specialist in that area.
- *Cultivate the marketing department* of your LLS establishment, or particular individuals who have responsibility for the public profile of the workplace. Offer to write a short article or press release outlining what you have been engaged in and the positive effects on learners. With the increasingly competitive LLS marketplace, senior managers are often keen to promote good news stories to attract funding, talented staff, and new learners.
- *Distil your knowledge.* Being able to condense your knowledge and experience into compact portions that quickly hook others in, as well as providing sound bites for publicity material or an article heading, will help communicate your key messages quickly and influentially.

Learning establishments often suffer from what can be termed a 'silo mentality'. Work is organized in tightly knit subject or programme units, and although this helps focus and manage activity, it does little for organizational learning. Cross-unit collaboration, with other departments, subject areas or geographical sites, can help the creative practitioner by strengthening weak ties in their internal network and building alliances with others (Hansen, 2009). For example, a tutor may have used a creative approach such as mind-mapping with a group of business learners but now is able to link with an engineering tutor who wishes to introduce such methods in their practice. The creative approach is taken out of the 'silo' to become a technique employed beneficially across the institution. The creativity café described in Chapter 9, 'Designing a Creative Session' (p. 98) would be an excellent way to bring tutors together.

As previously mentioned, internal publicity may not be sufficient. By networking externally, the creative practitioner has the opportunity to go beyond official hierarchies and structures to alliances of interests that may sway vital stakeholders (Kakabadse, 1991). By electronically communicating and networking, the creative tutor is potentially able to access a global online community:

- Email, discussion boards, blogs, podcasts, chat rooms, and video conferencing can enable interaction between the creative tutor and others. For instance, if a podcast has been stimulating, post a comment on the discussion board that often accompanies them.

- As in the internal context above, it is best to research the potential sources of support and knowledge. Hansen calls these the 'hubs' – the places where influential networking is already taking place. These may include subject-specific global (or local) discussion groups, professional associations and institutions, or centres of excellence attached to particular organizations. Increasingly, global portals for areas of interest, such as creativity, act as a repository for sharing resources, and also for engaging with other teaching and learning practitioners. These may have an accompanying wiki, where the community of users can freely create and edit content.

- Joining mailing lists can be very useful as a means of publicizing or disseminating information linked to creative endeavour, or for publicizing the results of action research.

- Spread your digital signature. Try to ensure that emails sent to others have a link embedded at the end of the message to work in progress, a recent publication, YouTube clip, or link to an organizational website.

- Creating a website, or a link to an existing organizational one, is time well spent. The website can be a valuable tool for showcasing the work the tutor and learners are engaged in, in visual and written form, as well as presenting the action research collaboratively carried out with colleagues. In addition, visitors can be encouraged to engage with tutors and offer their own experiences/questions/reactions. An accompanying blog can help to give an up-to-date record of progress, 'warts and all'. It is important for the website to be kept up to date so new visitors can assess the progress of the initiative.

- Establish a social networking platform. By creating a Facebook or Twitter account, the developer is able to utilize the bite-size chunks of knowledge and learning referred to above, then network using these popular platforms.

Each of these methods helps to establish and maintain a global presence on the web. They also offer the creative practitioner an opportunity to learn from others and gather information and knowledge to further the development of the particular practice initiative.

Even though video conferencing and chat can enable real-time dialogue, there is still great value in physically meeting up and engaging with other practitioners who are external to the practice context. Traditionally, the trade conference has provided such a forum. The increasing cost of attending a traditional conference, especially during times of increased pressure on staff development budgets, and the time spent away from the workplace, are factors that prevent many from attending. A well-run conference, however, can provide an excellent forum for the creative practitioner to listen, learn, and engage. Presenting a paper can be a daunting proposition for some. Nevertheless, if the presentation is showcased as work in progress, and the presenter(s) makes clear that they are eager to involve the audience in contributing to their learning, much can be gained. Outside of the main conference hall is where a great deal of the return on investment is made; through informal chats and shared meals, important relationships can be begun. The randomness and informality of a great deal of the communication often makes this form of networking superior to the stilted nature of a lot of electronic contact.

Not all face-to-face external contact has to be of the high-cost variety. Low-cost and effective forums exist. One of the authors has been a member of an action learning set for a number of years, which is part of a wider network in the UK. Here members meet up once a month to discuss shared current issues and decide upon actions, offer coaching and supervision, as well as share resources and knowledge appropriate to each other's practice. The ability to express ideas with practitioners outside of the immediate work setting often brings insightful comments, uncontaminated by organizational politics and narrow perspectives.

Throughout this chapter, we have sought to bolster the success of the planned change in practice, whether that is as an individual practitioner or a group of tutors. Core themes can be identified:

- Whenever embarking on change it is important to do the research. On p. 122 we encourage the tutor to look at their practice setting by employing the 7-S model.

- Similarly, the action research methodology leads the co-inquirers to engage in a critically reflective process that plans and then assesses agreed actions.
- We have also recognized the potential for resistance to new creative ideas. Overcoming such resistance can be a challenge. Employing a clear strategy, with identifiable and desirable outcomes that are well publicized, can win over many doubters.
- It can be a lonely and daunting task doing this alone. So fostering collaboration and involvement, including the learner voice, can help to support and challenge.
- Finally, the creative tutor is advised to reach out to the wider community of practitioners, both within and outside the practice context, so that energy and time are not wasted by well-intentioned but inescapably fruitless deeds. Moreover, internal stakeholders may pay heed to external opinion as to the worth of the change.

Developing creative approaches can be exciting, rewarding, and fun. Those practitioners trying to bring about a creative change in practice in certain learning settings may experience fewer positive thoughts and emotions than practitioners in other settings. This chapter has sought to ensure that, throughout the development journey, the positives outweigh the negatives.

11 Looking after the Creative Tutor

In Part 1 of this book, we emphasized the need for creative tutors to be aware of their wellbeing. This chapter highlights why this is necessary, and just what 'looking after' entails. We identify the particular stresses and strains of being a creative tutor, as well as the impact such tensions may have on them, their peers, and learners. It is our view that dealing with pressure is part of the professional role – critically reflecting and then acting on that reflection. The chapter concludes with practical advice on securing wellbeing for the creative tutor.

What we want to avoid from the outset is the notion that responsibility for wellbeing is solely down to the individual. Managers need to take a careful look at the workplaces that such tutors inhabit. Too often LLS organizations argue that the wellbeing of staff is a priority. The Human Resources function may provide 'stress management courses' for those in need, as though wellbeing can be secured through a short course. The message is quite clear: 'You are not coping, so here are some techniques to help you cope better'. As we have argued throughout this text, however, learning takes place in a context. Tutors are a vital component, but they are often reacting to decisions made outside their influence. These include:

- the way workload is allocated
- the support they receive, or the team they are a part of
- the management style adopted
- the quality assurance procedures, especially audits from external bodies such as Ofsted, which at certain times can place great pressure on tutors (and their managers).

Consequently, wellbeing is not just the individual tutor's responsibility but also an organization-wide issue. For creative tutors, we argue, wellbeing is even more important, and so they need to be aware whether it is being secured.

A definition of wellbeing that supports our holistic view of the creative tutor in a specific environment is that of Aelterman et al. (2007: 286):

> Wellbeing expresses a positive emotional state, which is the result of harmony between the sum of specific environmental factors on the one hand, and the personal needs and expectations of teachers on the other hand.

Here, the sense of balance between the learning context and what the individual desires and anticipates will determine wellbeing. The creative tutor has a number of desires, especially in an LLS setting. As with any tutor, it is hoped that learners are inspired by their practice. As argued in the first part of this book, however, the need for engagement of increasingly diverse learners places a responsibility on tutors to increasingly use creative methods. Such methods develop a sense of fun, novelty, and curiosity. They dispel the notion that the learner is passive, a sponge to soak up (to varying degrees) the knowledge imparted by the tutor. Here the learner is active, often working alongside peers and experiencing different learning approaches. Therefore, a creative tutor needs energy and space to generate new ideas and concepts of learning. There is a positive, confident attitude held by most creative tutors. They tend to be motivated by a passion to improve on the present, as well as a strong commitment to learner experience.

Such a pen portrait has a dark side. The pursuit of improvement and innovation can lead to 'busy-ness', with time for critical reflection squeezed by the need for action.

Thinking points

busy-ness = so busy looking down at the bustle of our everyday lives, that we don't have time or space to look up at who we are, or where we are going.

To what extent does this characterize your life at present?

Consequently, there can be a high risk of burnout as creative tutors push themselves too hard (Skovholt, 2001). Moreover, because these types of tutors tend to be different and wedded to innovation, new developments get pushed their way. This can be exciting and a sign that the tutor's work is appreciated. Yet, extra work leads to more deadlines and energy exerted. Expectations that they will deliver become heightened, and pressure can increase. Moreover, it is not always easy to spread the workload evenly throughout the year, as LLS settings tend to have a 'high season'.

The high season

This period may be characterized by the following:

- Programme beginnings where learners need to assimilate the new ways of working. Tutors working especially intensively to get groups of learners 'up and going'.

- Exam or assessment time when assessment by the tutor in whatever form can be laborious and stressful, especially if working with large groups.
- Internal or external quality inspections that may lead to more applications (and so greater funding to maintain jobs or resources) attracted by a high grade.

It is not surprising that, at these times, tutors can become stressed and exhausted, with potential for 'ill-being' (Huppert, 2010), which has consequences for both peers and significant others outside of the workplace.

In addition, this high season seems to be extending into other periods of the year, when traditionally tutors had been able to catch breath. The pace of work is seemingly more intense. So why has this pressure increased for those working in the Lifelong Learning Sector? A major reason has been changes in the working environment (Joseph, 2000). Further education, in particular, has undergone rapid change in the last decade. Until 1993, local authorities controlled further education colleges. However, 'incorporation' subsequently transferred staff, land, and other resources to new 'corporations', the FE colleges themselves. They became self-governed and were able to make substantial changes to the way in which they worked. Former contracts to staff were altered to extend the working year and hours worked, and so potentially increase college income and the flexibility of working. At one time colleges would close in July and then reopen in September with a recruitment period, whereas now pressure is placed on tutors to get the students recruited to programmes throughout the year and colleges rarely close.

The introduction of the marketplace – colleges competing for the same student in a given geographical area – has meant that tutors are carrying the burden of not only contributing to the education portfolio, but also satisfying the business case of their institution. Pressure to attract and, importantly, retain learners (funding is often linked to retention rates) has become paramount. Therefore, the rapidly evolving FE curriculum places demands on tutors to develop new programmes, compile written documentation to support them and materials for teaching, often during the summer months. It is not surprising that staff have begun to feel the stresses and strains of this expanded role. A survey carried out in 1997 showed increased stress levels since incorporation (Joseph, 2000) among FE staff, with associated tumbling levels in morale. A more recent survey in 2008 found that the situation had not changed (Court and Kinman, 2008). The stress levels of 3000 FE staff were found to exceed the average for British workers on seven key measures, as defined by the Health and Safety Executive (HSE), which analyses stress among the general working population. The seven measures are (HSE, 1995, 2001; Mackay et al., 2004):

1   Demands (e.g. workload, work patterns and the working environment)
2   Control (how much say the person has in the way they do their work)
3   Support (e.g. encouragement, sponsorship and resources provided by the organization, line management, and colleagues)
4   Relationships at work (e.g. promoting positive working practices to avoid conflict and dealing with unacceptable behaviour)
5   Role (whether people understand their role within the organization and whether the organization ensures that the person does not have conflicting roles)
6   Change (how organizational change – large or small – is managed and communicated in the organization)
7   Culture (management commitment and procedures that are fair and open).

More than half (55 per cent) reported 'high' or 'very high' general levels of stress. Furthermore, the survey found that prison tutors were even more stressed. Two-thirds of those surveyed experienced 'high' or 'very high' levels of stress. The constant retendering for education prison contracts creates instability and pressure to manage change effectively.

At the time of writing, a news report highlights the reduction in applications by students to UK universities. Many of the factors described above in relation to further education can also be found in the higher education sector. The reduction in government funding for universities has put pressure on institutions to raise student fees to meet the shortfall. With higher fees come higher learner expectations of what and how they are taught, while at the same time many faculties are increasing class size to raise revenues. Such pressures place heavy emphasis on tutors to satisfy learners' needs, which is not always easy when faced with large groups and limited time for preparation and learner support.

Such environmental pressures matter for the creative tutor. The busyness culture does not create time for reflection, preparation or discussion with others. Consequently, the conditions outlined earlier for creative working become constrained. The pressure to perform does not always help experimentation or team working, as colleagues play safe and focus on their own area of work. Or, if a team culture pervades, colleagues are frustrated because they want (or need) to meet – both formally and informally – but their energies get pulled elsewhere.

Yet, at the same time, the need to attract, retain, and engage learners is even greater. The latter can also be a problem for creative tutors. As they foster positive learning relationships in creative spaces through person-centred methods, learners recognize the value of creative, empathic tutors in enabling qualities and skills. Such rewards could be seen as a positive outcome of their work. Unfortunately, it can also lead to learners making greater demands on these tutors while colleagues, who are more distant, have less engagement, and therefore little impact on learners' progress. Thus, the authors have identified how learners can drain a creative tutor's time outside of the learning space, through demanding unreasonable face-to-face time, or instant replies to queries on a virtual learning space.

A key factor in securing wellbeing is therefore management of the creative tutor's time. As with relationship management in the classroom, discussed in Part 2, so the on-going support and contact with learners outside of this setting needs to be attended to. For example, setting clear ground rules if a virtual learning environment, such as Blackboard, is being used. The tutor needs to communicate to learners the times when they will be online to support their learning. The growth of mobile technology, such as tablets and mobile phones, that can access the Internet on the move, ensures that learners and tutors can, in theory, make learning a 24/7 activity. The tutor has to ensure that they manage time effectively to provide a healthy work–life balance. Later in this chapter, in the 'Tree of Wellbeing' section (p. 147), suggestions will be provided as to how this may be secured.

Despite many of the pressures mentioned above, creative work does take place within LLS settings. Notwithstanding the 'value for money' paradigm that pervades so much of the sector, tutors are finding ways to deal with frustration and develop new ways of engaging with learners. Our own position is that such practice will no longer be the actions of a 'lone-ranger' tutor – one who excites and innovates alongside learners, but who is set apart from colleagues who lack the knowledge, skills or inclination, to follow suit. Teams of tutors will need to work together to ensure engagement is a common factor across a learner's experience of a programme, or across different parts of the organization. Therefore, the issue of wellbeing becomes a collective task, looking after each other, as distinct from purely looking after oneself.

Being professional

In the previous chapter, the importance of critical reflection of professional practice was highlighted (p. 126). Here we wish to bring the same thinking to the wellbeing sphere. It is our contention that, as a professional, the creative tutor needs to identify their current skills and competences, while at the same time thinking ahead to how the learning space is evolving. In response, the tutor needs to consider what is going to assist them to keep abreast of change and thrive. Thus, securing wellbeing becomes an integral facet of their professional development.

Not all tutors in the Lifelong Learning Sector have a permanent post in an organization. The sector contains many freelance, self-employed or part-time tutors, involved in learning and development, in a whole variety of public and private sector organizations. These 'lone workers' also have to be professional in terms of securing wellbeing.

Thinking points

If you are a 'lone worker', as described above, how do you ensure your wellbeing? How do you secure your health and safety, for example, where you work? Do you have an effective procedure to enable productive contracting and payment for your services?

Lone workers can often be the 'forgotten shift':

- Due to their contractual arrangements, which are often based on contact hours with learners, their visibility within an organization may be limited.
- A feeling of isolation can easily develop.
- Lone workers may be marginalized, especially in terms of access to resources, or joint working and development that full-time staff may enjoy.
- Knowledge of, and access to, services such as human resources or additional management support, may be restricted by part-time status.

One of the authors remembers facilities being available for part-time staff in a college where they could mix with others of the same status, and so feel less adrift of the main teaching staff. Unfortunately, however, the institution decided to reorganize due to financial stringency and the part-time facility was the first to be cut. As a result, full-time staff and learners contacted the part-time staff by email; the latter entering the building and going straight to the teaching classroom, and then leaving once their class contact was over. Consequently, such workers need to be resilient, and possibly more reliant and aware of their wellbeing than full-time employees.

To use a metaphor – using a computer can be frustrating, as the operative has to deal with continual software updates that need to be acknowledged and acted upon. Yet, these developments enable the machine to cope with potentially damaging viruses, and remedy the faults that often occur with fast-paced technological change. A smooth-running machine results in a happy, contented operative. Similarly, the professional tutor can contribute to their own wellbeing by considering the potential hazards and glitches that may upset the balance between their environment and personal needs and aspirations.

One of the common complaints of practitioners is the pace of change in the Lifelong Learning Sector. Thus, one strategy could be to take a professional stance, to 'be ahead of the game'.

Thinking points

Looking to the future, what might be the ways your own practice will change? Could new technological advances, for example, impact significantly on what, and how, your learners engage with your area of study? Or could it be shifts in what different stakeholders, such as employers, expect from your learners?

Another metaphor using cars would be: a good driver not only has quick reactions for the unexpected but anticipates *what might happen*, and adjusts their driving as a result. Low temperatures or foggy conditions demand a reduction in speed, so the driver can brake quickly and safely if necessary. There is a need for balance here. Consider what it is like to be a passenger with a driver who is over-cautious and sees potential danger everywhere, so is constantly jabbing the brakes causing the passenger (and anyone following them) to feel highly uncomfortable. Similarly, the creative tutor needs to *realistically* think ahead – reading their own practice road – to gain an understanding of possible new developments, in both their own subject area and the wider social and political context. For example, an FE college is forging links with a local school, so that learners over 14 years can access some of the college courses that the school is unable to offer. A tutor in that college would need to assess the different demands of learners at 14 years of age, compared with the adults who make up the majority of their current teaching timetable. The tutor could then critically reflect on areas of their practice they may need to develop, such as improved classroom management, or liaising with external organizations.

The above example is a quite specific demand and the tutor can be proactive in meeting it. Not all change, with attendant impact, is so identifiable. The introduction of new technology and its impact on various areas of a tutor's practice is a good example of a more universal trend. Electronic assessment methods are now widespread across the Lifelong Learning Sector. The shift from piles of scripts to a candidate's online submission can be a daunting one for tutors who are not so IT-savvy, or who fail to regularly back up their work for fear the IT system crashes.

Similarly, the proliferation of Web 2.0 technology – blogs, wikis, social networking, and video-sharing applications – where content is created by the users, as opposed to their being consumers of content directed at them, is being embraced by educators and trainers. Although tutors may not have a personal blog or social networking accounts, it is important to be aware of the potential for learners to generate content and increase interaction with peers, and other learners, across the globe. Some creative tutors will use such technologies to enhance engagement and learning. The speed of such developments, however, can be daunting. Consequently, learning from users can be most worthwhile. Asking a receptive and knowledgeable learner about the latest trends and their use can sometimes be more productive than a day of staff development. Such an approach can be extended to form a useful group activity. The tutor may find that they are unsure about how a wiki could help students' collaboration. The group could be tasked with setting up such a site, within the parameters of the organization's policy on such use, then reviewing the effectiveness of the wiki for their learning after a period of time.

Equally, the message boards of professional associations can generate valuable links to content and shared experience of what boosts creativity. The UK's Institute for Learning (IfL) is a useful hub for boosting professional development. It offers sector information and links, providing online communities for the FE and skills sector, with a commitment to influencing policy within the Lifelong Learning Sector. Members of IfL can share experiences, tips, and resources. These links are valuable for tutors, especially those who find their own learning setting resistant to change. Being in touch with others who have achieved small or large shifts in practice can boost confidence, helping tutors overcome the struggle that may characterize their current working practice.

Due to the scope of the changes outlined above, the creative tutor needs to be cautious. There is a danger of trying to develop too much, with so many developmental opportunities, especially via the Internet, to extend both subject knowledge and skills to enhance learning spaces. By scoping the practice field and assessing needs – in the short, medium, and long term – the creative tutor can construct a realistic development strategy that keeps them abreast of change. Moreover, this targeting process helps to ameliorate the sense that they are not in control of the shifting landscape of their practice, and thus helps avoid wasting valuable time and energy on just trying to 'keep up to date'. In this way, the creative tutor is using a professional stance to enhance their wellbeing.

Practitionerself: the novice and experienced

One of the authors can remember distinctly when on their first teaching placement the door closed, and they were introduced to the class by the experienced teacher before he left. The group looked up at the novice teacher and waited. That pause seemed to go on forever. Suddenly they realized that they were in charge of the class and everything that went on within that space. Professional training and instinct kicked in and the anxiety started to recede slightly. The learners responded and confidence was boosted. As a novice tutor, the 'fragile and incomplete practitionerself shifts through a series of moods: elation, fear, relief, frustration, delight, despair, pride and shame' (Skovholt, 2001: 74). Moreover, the novice tutor tends to stick to a rigid, prescribed role and function. The aim is to persuade others that you can pass through the opening to professional status. Once that has been achieved, the creative tutor's practice becomes a process of shedding and adding:

> trying out a wide variety of methods, approaches, and techniques; insights from direct and indirect feedback from clients, students and patients; learning from supervisors and other professional 'elders'; and learning from admired peers.
>
> (Skovholt, 2001: 44)

The above discussion is relevant to wellbeing. The feeling of responsibility may never evaporate, but it tends to be managed better by more experienced tutors. The ability and confidence to try out different methods and grow a distinct creative style comes with experience and a willingness to reflect and learn (in Chapter 3, 'Confidence and Creativity' (p. 23), we discuss the main components of confidence and why it is important for the creative tutor). Yet, as the above recognizes, the stage of development of a tutor is critical in how they cope. Some tutors never learn all of these lessons. The current challenge of teaching in the Lifelong Learning Sector is not for the faint-hearted. The future challenges of engagement and diversity will place greater emphasis on coping and managing self, even for the most experienced. The recurring theme of this chapter is that, to be a creative tutor, it is necessary to look after your 'practitionerself' and others.

The novice tutor may enter a practice setting fresh from their training, or may be on placement as part of their teaching qualification. Casting an eye around at colleagues and their practices can be illuminating. Initially, it may be assumed that all the experienced tutors are coping and employing highly effective methods of engaging their learners. This belief may be shattered, however, once they are observed at close quarters, or learners' critical conversations are overheard about a previous session. Expertise is not necessarily increased by length of tenure. Earlier, the notion of 'reading the practice road' to be prepared for new developments was stressed. The driving metaphor can be extended here to explore the experience of a creative novice tutor.

One of the authors learnt to drive with an excellent instructor. After they had passed their driving test their father would often accompany them, the latter now in the unusual position of passenger. The novice driver had been taught well, but was constantly berated by comments of 'you don't need to do that' or 'why has he taught you that?' The father had been driving for many years, developed his own 'unique' style, and was trying to influence the emerging technique of the novice. It took some resilience to ignore the passenger, as well as the temptation to stop the car, open the door and let them walk!

For the novice creative tutor, such resilience is equally important for their wellbeing. They may enter a practice setting with lots of ideas and activities they know have worked well in their training. In addition, they have their own vision of their new creative learning setting. It is important for them to filter out the potential negativity of colleagues who may have a different, possibly cynical, vision of learning and 'how it should be done'.

One of the authors was mentoring a new tutor in a college setting teaching Business Studies. The novice was astounded to hear the reaction of a college tutor to the creative approaches they had in mind, which would encourage involvement of the learners at the beginning of a session. The experienced tutor at the college was advising them to 'just stick them on the computers and get them going on their assignment'. The novice intended to get the group thinking about the assignment title, and how they might tackle it through a mind-mapping exercise. Small groups were then to feed back to the tutor and peers their puzzles and queries, before they embarked on the assignment.

Thankfully, for the learners and the tutor, the tutor decided to follow their convictions and went ahead with the planned session. It was a success, with the learners saying how much they had valued the thinking and discussion time before embarking on the assignment. Now they were keen to get started on it. The tutor absorbed the feedback and gained confidence in acting on their own instincts. Possibly, the more negative tutor had always taught in the same way, not opening up to new possibilities and unwilling to listen to feedback on their methods. This is not the way to sustain creative professional growth.

We are not saying the comments of more experienced tutors should be completely ignored. The novice may be embarking on something that is completely inappropriate and needs to think again. Having this sense of openness to others' views is healthy. Such views need to be reflected on, then considered as being worthy of attention or not. Just as with the father booming across to the driver what they should or should not be doing, a consideration of whether others' views are valid or just predilections is the way forward. Moreover, it is hoped that novice tutors find themselves in an open, supportive work environment, where negativity and cynicism are in short supply. Unfortunately, this is not always the case.

Three ways to enhance the professional creative potential of the tutor are to:

- have a sense and acknowledgement of the creative self
- have the courage and skills to apply methods generated by it
- employ a reflective process.

Overall, we have sought to position wellbeing as an integral part of being professional. It is also recognized that novice creative practice needs to be nurtured and developed. Engaging in self-care is important for wellbeing, especially during stressful periods in the tutor's life. Furthermore, the wellbeing of the tutor will also ensure the learners are benefiting from creative learning spaces. Without a nurtured creative tutor, the learners face potentially uninspiring and unproductive learning experiences. Again, we return to one of the key themes of the book – creativity as being relational: 'the space between'. In this respect, being professional in terms of securing wellbeing enhances that space between, for the benefit of both tutor and learners.

The Tree of Wellbeing

Up to this point, the chapter has located wellbeing in the practice and organizational context of the tutor. However, our lives – the hopes and fears, experiences, relationships, sense of self – are rarely so bounded. The tutor does not leave the rest of their existence at the entrance to work and pick it up again at home time. Practice experiences may be punctuated by thoughts and feelings, reflections and actions that have their source outside of the confines of the learning space. So securing wellbeing for the creative tutor needs to embrace 'being' in its total sense. For example, in a very practical sense, constant lack of sleep is likely to impair performance in the learning space.

Many researchers in the wellbeing field include some form of diagnostic tool to explore what 'being well' would mean for the reader. Such tools often involve a sense of balancing of varying facets of life. For example, the physical, emotional, spiritual, intellectual components of our lives are scored or assessed, at any one time, to understand how they are helping or hindering our wellbeing. Such a 'balance' is an illusion, as well as potentially harmful, because it sets unrealistic expectations of practitioners, at a time when work is becoming more intense and demanding (Harvey, 2010). To have an imbalance between 'work' and 'life' is deemed to be a sign of not coping. Yet to practise in the Lifelong Learning Sector often crosses such divides. Work is sometimes brought home; vital physical workspace is created, where possible, to cope with these demands. The spread of fast broadband and wireless Internet connections, as well as smartphone technology, means that there can be a constant link between home and work. There are times in the year, and career of the practitioner, when work does become extremely demanding, and trying to achieve a balance is mere fantasy. Similarly, home demands may impinge on work time. For example, caring for elderly parents at times of crisis or looking after a sick child demands one's complete attention. The tutor manages at these times by drawing on own strengths and of those around them. It is these assets their that assist and nurture our wellbeing, especially when we are under pressure, for a whole variety of reasons. Recognizing these, and then seeking ways to nourish them, is vital for wellbeing.

Figure 11.1, the Tree of Wellbeing, shows the main elements of wellbeing for the creative tutor. The reader is encouraged to consider each element of the Tree in turn, and reflect on what is important for them.

The trunk. These are the core ideals that serve to motivate and are at the centre of both your practice and other parts of your life. You may consider such ideals as respect for the learner and yourself as a professional practitioner, or fairness, equality, and self-expression for everyone in the learning space. Whatever your ideals, they are important and at the core of your wellbeing, as they support all the other elements that 'branch off' from them. The core can be recognized in how you develop your creative practice, whoever is in that learning space.

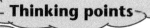

Thinking points

So, which ideals are at the centre of your practice?

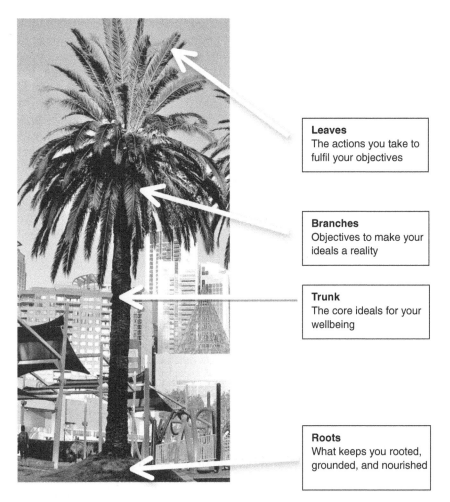

Leaves
The actions you take to
fulfil your objectives

Branches
Objectives to make your
ideals a reality

Trunk
The core ideals for your
wellbeing

Roots
What keeps you rooted,
grounded, and nourished

Figure 11.1 The Tree of Wellbeing

The branches. The core ideals that underpin your practice and life need to be realized in some form so as to maintain your wellbeing. Thus if a core belief is the importance of self-expression, the learning session will need to be organized to ensure that all learners have the opportunity to contribute. Learners have to recognize that ground rules are in place to ensure that self-expression is not abused to the detriment of others, including the tutor. We have stressed throughout that finding time to prepare and consider creative approaches is a key attribute of the creative tutor in the Lifelong Learning Sector. One possible branch of wellbeing would be for the tutor to consider how they secure such a creative space. Another essential core ideal would be personal development. Consequently, its respective branch of wellbeing may contain plans that are realistic for that tutor's stage of development and demands on other areas of their life. So, for example, a tutor studying for their part-time Masters in Education must ensure that the Wednesday evening trip to the cinema with their partner is protected in the diary, as is the weekend sports fixture with their young family. At the heart lies the core; what is important for that individual guides how they wish to be. Individual circumstances will influence such planning. A good manager or mentor will help to guide a creative tutor to ensure that such plans are realized. The wellbeing of the employee or mentee needs to be part of their guidance agenda. Placing ever increasing developmental demands on the tutor when it is going to have an adverse impact on his or her wellbeing is not going to serve either party. The creative tutor's performance will be affected, with a potential negative impact on physical and mental health.

Thinking points

So, what are your branches? What do you do to ensure that what you truly believe in gets realized, both at work and in the rest of your life?

The leaves. These are the actions attached to your branches. Each branch, the objective that stems from the trunk, contains individual day-to-day actions that contribute to wellbeing. As each one is achieved, it 'falls' from the branch. Gather these up at the end of the session to determine if you have achieved them. Such positive actions accumulate at the base of the trunk and over time will cumulatively act as 'mulch' to nourish those ideals.

Thinking points

Take a typical day and consider which of your actions contributed to your wellbeing?

The roots. Thus, we have established the core ideals, the trunk of your tree. Stemming from these will be ways in which they can be realized, the branches. Each branch will have leaves, the individual actions that you and others take to achieve the various facets of wellbeing. But what are the roots of this tree? What will help sustain you? What will keep you rooted and grounded? For some, it may be the support of a partner or mentor who encourages, stimulates, challenges, and grounds the person when the turbulence above ground threatens to uproot the trunk. For others, it may be their faith or political beliefs. Such roots need nourishment. As suggested, the accumulation of positive actions to sustain wellbeing can be nourishing in themselves. The positive feedback from learners, or observations of 'making a difference' to individuals or whole groups, can be self-sustaining. However, the roots can sometimes be ignored, taken for granted, with consequent effects on the individual sustaining what they consider important.

Thinking points

So, what are the roots that nourish your wellbeing? How do you acknowledge their importance to you?

To this point, all the elements of wellbeing have had a positive slant. If only lives, both professional and personal, were all so nourishing and full of growth! At the risk of felling this metaphor, other elements can be identified that may threaten such an optimistic view of achieving wellbeing.

Fungus. The perils of the tree (or it's protector in the environment?). What is the creeper in the tutor's professional and personal lives that may strangle this tree and cut off its life?

The potential of the forest. Throughout we have embraced the notion of nourishing the creative tutor, as well as the realistic expectation that practice settings are not always so fertile or encouraging. Wellbeing should not be a sole pursuit for the creative tutor. Trees gain protection from elements as a collective; young saplings and branches gain from being with others. Such is the role of colleagues and significant others that share the creative tutor's life. With access to professional and personal networks, the tutor's forest can have a global reach. Knowing that others share the core ideals and are realizing these on a day-to-day basis in their work and rest of their lives can be potentially a great support and valuable resource. Hopefully, the creative tutor will have such a forest close to home – when they enter practice settings and when they leave them.

Conclusion

In this chapter, we have sought to locate wellbeing within the professional practice of the creative tutor. In particular, the LLS context of the full-time and 'lone worker' has been explored to ensure that wellbeing is not detached from the practice setting in which it is trying to be secured. Creative tutors have particular needs to ensure that they have space and sustenance to secure the novelty, engagement, curiosity, and fun that learning settings in the Lifelong Learning Sector require. Thus, wellbeing becomes not just an individual quest, but also an organizational issue, involving tutors, learners, and managers. As Juniper (2012) has remarked, if you want to improve the performance of a car, you have to first look under the bonnet. So job design, workspace, and how creative tutors are managed become critical issues. How can we secure creativity in LLS learning settings if the architecture, in both a physical and a managerial sense, is not in place? Organizations within the sector need to examine carefully how their current provision on both these accounts helps or hinders the creative tutor's wellbeing.

Nevertheless, to focus purely on the individual and the organizational context is not enough if we are going to secure wellbeing. Huppert (2010: 1276) comments that:

> First, the creation of well-being requires more than the remediation of problems – this merely reduces ill-being. It requires that the whole population is shifted towards flourishing. Second, sustainable happiness results from what we do, not what we have; we need to be able to create our own well-being and contribute to that of others. Third, we cannot assume that translating the evidence into interventions will produce a flourishing society; we must commit to rigorous evaluation to find out what works, for whom, for how long, for which outcomes and in what contexts. Happiness breeds prosperity.

The above resonates on a number of levels in relation to what we have discussed so far. First, Huppert suggests that only by having a focus on 'flourishing' can we have the foundation for wellbeing. The creative tutor could argue that their intent is to contribute to such flourishing by engendering a sense of engagement with learning, a thirst for curiosity, and a realization that learning spaces can be fun and worthwhile. The 'Five Ways to Well-Being', identified by the New Economics Foundation (2008), feature both 'learning' and 'taking notice' as two of the five evidence-based ways to secure wellbeing. Being involved in learning leads to confidence and fun. Taking notice and being curious results in conscious wellbeing. Alternatively, a more critical view would be that Huppert's creation of wellbeing is hard to achieve during austere times, with unequal access to the resources that might enhance the development of the individual. At the time of the writing, the possibility of a 'whole nation' flourishing seems pretty remote with cuts to funding and reduced resources.

Second, the need to create our own wellbeing is at the heart of this chapter, especially alongside others. By identifying the various components that make up the tutor's 'Tree of Wellbeing', we have adopted a relational approach to identify what is important in both professional and personal life, and how it can be secured and nourished in conjunction with others.

Lastly, the chapter offers a guide for the creative tutor, to encourage exploration and evaluation of the ideas we have put forward. Wellbeing is highly subjective, peculiar to individuals in certain circumstances at any one time. Those conditions can change, especially when creating (and being created by) learning spaces that are often beset with ambiguity and unpredictability. Only by carefully examining the environmental factors at any one time, and how these match – or not – with the personal needs and expectations of the creative tutor, will harmony between professional and personal lives be attained.

Epilogue: The Currency of Creativity

This book encourages tutors to explore new ways of engaging learners, based on a belief of what stimulates, excites, and involves. Learners benefit as well as tutors and, as a consequence, so do the organizations where they practise. We also feel strongly that it is time to redress the balance of learning and the dominant discourses of the last twenty years in the Lifelong Learning Sector. The dins of accountability, funding, and quality assurance have drowned out talk of lifelong learning. Much is spoken of the need to re-engage young people with education and training, but little about how and what will be practised. The danger is that a variety of institutions will resort to providing the same fare that put (young) people off learning in the first place.

We have also sought to represent the creative tutor as a valuable resource. Creative tutors possess the mindset and skills to excite and stimulate discovery. Therefore, creative practice can be seen as a currency. It provides the tutor with a powerful mechanism for enabling change and crossing boundaries in their career. At one time, the notion of success in a teaching career was a linear passage within, or between, similar institutions. Effective tutors gained promotion within their own institution (and sadly, as they obtained more senior positions, became further removed from the learner), or they moved to another similar institution that offered a promotion opportunity. With increased reorganization of the Lifelong Learning Sector, these pathways may no longer exist as institutions merge or are realigned. The expansion of the sector has also offered new opportunities with new providers, flexible working arrangements, and new choices to be made by tutors to enhance employability, such as the use of transferable skills to enter consultancy or training. Therefore, creative approaches now have a currency across a wider range of potential learning settings, within the tutor's own locale, or across the globe.

Thus, if creativity has such a value, it needs to be invested wisely. We have stressed the need for creative tutors to take care of their own wellbeing. Deciding when and where to invest energy is important in order to avoid burnout. By adopting a professional stance to looking after the creative self, the tutor is able to explore the challenges that lie ahead, then assess and develop the skills and competences to meet and exploit such challenges. Valuable currency also does not tend to be discarded wastefully but is kept in a secure place. Therefore, securing and retaining the value of creative approaches is an organizational issue, not just the responsibility of the individual tutor. The management of practice settings needs to reflect how well they are providing support for such a valuable resource. An effective currency investment company regularly assesses its portfolio to ensure that the maximum return is being secured for its clients. Similarly, managers of practice settings need to review to what extent they are providing recognition, support, challenge, and potential development for creative tutors.

Currency is also circulated and used. This book has highlighted the possibilities in sharing practice with others. So much can be gained from tapping into creative networks that can encourage critical reflection, supply new ideas and resources, support and encouragement. It can be argued that this is all well and good, but how can time be found for such activity when faced with a full timetable of work, a burgeoning email inbox, and assessments to be completed? There is no doubt that work has intensified for a profession that traditionally has shouldered an administrative load, in addition to the core activity of engaging with learners. Yet there is a danger of becoming too inwardly focused and not reaching out to beyond the immediate practice setting. Good practice is not shared and the tutor's learning, in the face of increasing demands on skills and competences, becomes stilted. Therefore, engaging with others is to be seen as part of professional practice. It becomes 'soul food' – boosting confidence and giving a wider perspective. In this way, creative tutors have to 'live creativity', not just provide it. They are learners too.

We hope the reader is beginning to see the sheen on their valuable currency. We hope their line managers, senior executives, and commissioners get a glimpse of this true value too. But we are also not so naive as to run away with the idea that all in the LLS garden is rosy. A trainee tutor may leave with their qualification all buoyed up with a kit bag of new ideas, and the confidence and zeal to employ them with diverse groups of learners. Nevertheless, they could take up a post that is not what it seemed based on the application form and interview. Their heart may sink as they seek to get by as best as they can. In this situation, resilience is important and self-talk that seeks to affirm the creative self – 'within the circumstances I am still creative and doing the best I can' – can help to withstand those pressures that stifle creative approaches. Employing the 'Trojan Mouse' strategy described in Chapter 10, 'Stimulating Creative Change in your

Practice' (p. 123), will help focus the strategy to what is manageable and achievable in that practice setting. Using publicity, especially involving your learners, who are often your most powerful allies in changing others' opinions, can engage with potential stakeholders outside of the practice setting and help the cause of change. Plant your 'Tree of Wellbeing' and keep it well mulched with creative actions, however small, that are accomplished and fall like leaves, thus nourishing new ideas and actions. Such approaches will help sustain belief in the value of the currency of creativity.

Lastly, the value of creativity is not just banked by the tutor but is in constant exchange with learners. What is developed in 'the space between' – that potential mint of a creative space between tutors, learners, and their peers – fashions value for learners that is not only focused on employability, but also for investing in learning for life. Employability therefore becomes part of lifelong learning, not distinct from it. The ability to think imaginatively, to be curious and ask questions, to engage with others, and see the learning potential of that involvement for both parties, all are valuable attributes in a workplace and economy (and life) that is constantly evolving. The LLS learner deserves that that currency, generated by their involvement, should be worth something. By adopting creative approaches to learning, that process for living a richer and more valuable life has begun, both inside and outside of work, for the LLS tutor and their learners.

References

Aelterman, A., Engels, N., Van Petegem, K. and Verhaeghe, J.P. (2007) The well-being of teachers in Flanders: the importance of a supportive school culture, *Educational Studies*, 33(3): 285–97.

Arpin-Cribbie, C.A. and Cribbie, R.A. (2007) Psychological correlates of fatigue: examining depression, perfectionism, and automatic negative thoughts, *Personality and Individual Differences*, 43(6): 1310–20.

Avis, J., Fisher, R. and Thompson, R. (2009) *Teaching in Lifelong Learning: A Guide to Theory and Practice*. Maidenhead: Open University Press.

Biggs, J. (2003) *Teaching for Quality Learning at University*, 2nd edn. Maidenhead: Open University Press.

Blatchford, P., Kutnick, P., Baines, E. and Galton, M. (2003) Toward a social pedagogy of classroom group work, *International Journal of Educational Research*, 39: 153–72.

Bohm, D. (1998) *On Creativity* (edited by L. Nichol). London: Routledge.

Bourne, L. and Walker, D. (2008) Project relationship management and the Stakeholder Circle™, *International Journal of Managing Projects in Business*, 1(1): 125–30.

Brookfield, S. (1995) Becoming critically reflective: a process of learning and change, in *Becoming a Critically Reflective Teacher*. San Francisco, CA: Jossey-Bass.

Burns, G. (1987) A typology of 'hooks' in popular records, *Popular Music*, 6(1): 1–20.

Coghlan, D. and Brannick, T. (2005) *Doing Action Research in Your Own Organisation*. London: Sage.

Cotton, T. (2011) From voice to choice: evaluation and action research into creativity, in P. Thompson and J. Sefton-Green (eds.) *Researching Creative Teaching*. London: Routledge.

Court, S. and Kinman, G. (2008) *Tackling Stress in Further Education*. London: UCU Publications.

Craft, A., Jeffrey, B. and Leibling, M. (eds.) (2001) *Creativity in Education.* London: Continuum.

Cropley, A. (2001) *Creativity in Education and Learning: A Guide for Teachers and Educators.* London: Kogan Page.

Davies, P. (2003) *Increasing Confidence.* London: Dorling Kindersley.

De Bono, E. (1995) *Parallel Thinking.* London: Penguin.

Duckett, I. and Tatarkowski, M. (2005) *Practical Strategies for Learning and Teaching on Vocational Programmes.* London: Learning and Skills Development Agency.

Eastwood, L., Coates, J., Dixon, I., Harvey, J., Ormondroyd, C. and Williamson, S. (2009) *A Toolkit for Creative Teaching in Post Compulsory Education.* Maidenhead: Open University Press.

Fautley, M. and Savage, J. (2007) *Creativity in Secondary Education.* Exeter: Learning Matters.

Gardener, H. (1993) *Frames of Mind: The Theories of Multiple Intelligences,* 2nd edn. London: Fontana Press.

Gibson, H. (2005) What creativity isn't: the presumptions of instrumental and individual justification for creativity in education, *British Journal of Education Studies,* 53(2): 148–67.

Gilliam, T. (2012) *On ideas, unlearning and avoiding debt.* Available at: http://the99percent.com/articles/7121/Terry-Gilliam-On-Ideas-Unlearning-Avoiding-Debt (accessed 16 January 2012).

Ginnis, P. (2005) *The Teacher's Toolkit: Promoting Variety, Engagement, and Motivation in the Classroom,* Vol. 1. Norwalk, CT: Crown House Publishing.

Grunfield, N. (2006) *The Big Book of Me: Become Your Own Life Coach.* London: Short Books.

Hanley, L. (2008) *Estates: An Intimate History.* London: Granta Books.

Hansen, M.T. (2009) *Collaboration: How Leaders Avoid the Traps, Create Unity, and Reap Big Results.* Boston, MA: Harvard Business School Press.

Harvey, B. (2007) Chuck out the chintz? 'Stripped floor' writing and the catalogue of convention: alternative perspectives on management inquiry, in K. Trehan, C. Rigg and J. Stewart (eds.) *Beyond Critical HRD.* London: Pearson.

Harvey, B. (2010) *Empowering lives through work–life balance – a critique.* Conference paper for the International Conference on Personal and Public Lives: Exploring Relationships, Roles and Responsibilities, University of Huddersfield, September 2010.

Harvey, J. (2009) Welcome to the creativity cafe: developing a network of shared creative teaching practice amongst academic staff, in A. Jackson (ed.) *Innovations and Development in Initial Teacher Education.* A selection of conference papers presented at the 4th Annual ESCalate ITE Conference, University of Cumbria, 16 May 2008. Bristol: ESCalate.

Health and Safety Executive (HSE) (1995) *Stress at Work: A Guide for Employers*. HS(G)116. Sudbury: HSE Books.

Health and Safety Executive (HSE) (2001) *Tackling Work-related Stress: A Managers' Guide to Improving and Maintaining Employee Health and Well-Being*. Sudbury: HSE Books.

Hot Potatoes™ Version 6 (undated) Available at: http://hotpot.uvic.ca/ (accessed 28 March 2012).

Huppert, F. (2010) Happiness breeds prosperity, *Nature*, 464: 1275–6.

Joseph, R. (2000) *Stress Free Teaching: A Practical Guide to Tackling Stress in Teaching, Lecturing and Tutoring*. London: Kogan Page.

Juniper, B. (2012) *Who should manage employee wellbeing?* Available at: http://www.personneltoday.com/articles/2012/01/09/58182/who-should-manage-employee-wellbeing.html (accessed 30 March 2012).

Kakabadse, A. (1991) Politics and ethics in action research, in N. Craig Smith and P. Dainty (eds.) *The Management Research Handbook*. London: Routledge.

Kemmis, S. and McTaggart, R. (1988) *The Action Research Planner*, 3rd edn. Geelong, VIC: Deakin University Press.

Lather, P. (1991) *Getting Smart: Feminist Research and Pedagogy Within/In the Postmodern*. New York: Routledge.

Light, G., Cox, R. and Calkins, S. (2009) *Learning and Teaching in Higher Education: The Reflective Professional*, 2nd edn. London: Sage.

Mackay, C., Cousins, R., Kelly, P., Lee, S. and McCaig, R. (2004) 'Management standards' and work-related stress in the UK: policy background and science, *Work and Stress*, 18: 91–112.

Manning, P. and Ray, G. (1993) Shyness, self-confidence and social interaction, *Social Psychology Quarterly*, 56(3): 178–92.

McNiff, J. and Whitehead, J. (2009) *Doing and Writing Action Research*. London: Sage.

Mosley, P. (2011) *Make Your Creativity Pay*. Worthing: Craft and Design.

National Advisory Committee on Creative and Cultural Education (NACCCE) (1999) *All Our Future: Creativity, Culture and Education*. London: DfEE Publications.

New Economics Foundation (NEF) (2008) *Five ways to wellbeing*. Available at: http://www.neweconomics.org/publications/five-ways-to-wellbeing (accessed 30 March 2012).

Norman, M. and Hyland, T. (2003) The role of confidence in lifelong learning, *Educational Studies*, 29(2/3): 261–72.

Oreskovic, A. (2012) *YouTube hits 4 billion daily video views*. Available at http://www.reuters.com/article/2012/01/23/us-google-youtube-idUSTRE80MOTS20120123 (accessed 24 September 2012).

Peters, T. and Waterman, R.H. (1982) *In Search of Excellence*. New York: Harper & Row.

Petrie, P., Boddy, J., Cameron, C., Wigfall, V. and Simon, A. (2006) *Working with Children in Care*. Maidenhead: Open University Press.

Petrie, P., Boddy, J., Cameron, C., Heptinstall, E., McQuail, S., Simon, A. and Wigfall, V. (2009) *Pedagogy – a holistic, personal approach to work with children and young people, across services*. Briefing Paper, Thomas Coram Research Unit (TCRU), Institute of Education, University of London. Available at: http://eprints.ioe.ac.uk/58/1/may_18_09_Ped_BRIEFING_PAPER_JB_PP_.pdf (accessed 22 March 2012).

Petty, G. (1998) *Teaching Today*. Cheltenham: Stanley Thornes.

Petty, G. (2009) *Teaching Today: A Practical Guide*, 4th edn. Cheltenham: Nelson Thornes.

Powell, R. (1997) *Active Whole-Cass Teaching*. Stafford: Robert Powell Publications.

Reason, P. (1994) *Participation in Human Inquiry*. London: Sage.

Reason, P. (1999) Integrating action and reflection through co-operative inquiry, *Management Learning*, 30(2): 207–27.

Reason, P. and Rowan, J. (eds.) (1981) *Human Inquiry: A Sourcebook of New Paradigm Research*. New York: Wiley.

Robinson, K. (2010) *The Element: How Finding Your Passion Changes Everything*. London: Penguin.

Rogers, C. (1969) *Freedom to Learn: A View of What Education Might Become*. Columbus, OH: Charles E. Merrill.

Schon, D. (1997) *Educating the Reflective Practitioner*. San Francisco, CA: Jossey-Bass.

Simmons, R. and Thompson, R. (2008) Creativity and performativity: the face of further education, *British Educational Research Journal*, 34(5): 601–18.

Skovholt, T.M. (2001) *The Resilient Practitioner*. Boston, MA: Allyn & Bacon.

Walker, D., Bourne, L. and Shelley, A. (2008) Influence, stakeholder mapping and visualization, *Construction Management and Economics*, 26(6): 645–58.

Weil, S. (1998) Rhetorics and realities in public service organisations: systemic practice and organisational learning as critically reflexive action research (CRAR), *Systemic Practice and Action Research*, 11(1): 37–62.

Wenger, E. (1998) *Communities of Practice: Learning, Meaning and Identity*. Cambridge: Cambridge University Press.

Index

IAN RUSHTON AND MARTIN SUTER

REFLECTIVE PRACTICE FOR TEACHING IN LIFELONG LEARNING

REFLECTIVE PRACTICE FOR TEACHING IN LIFELONG LEARNING

Ian Rushton and Martin Suter

9780335244010 (Paperback)
2012

eBook also available

"The authors set out to produce a book that would "demystify reflective practice" and they have succeeded!!! The book is rich in practical wisdom, concisely expressed, and will enable both experienced teachers and new entrants to use reflective practice to improve and develop teaching and learning in a complex and diverse lifelong learning sector."
Dr David Holloway, University of Portsmouth, UK.

Key features:

- Designed to address the needs of student teachers in the Lifelong Learning Sector (LLS) across a whole range of courses
- Illustrated by real examples drawn from the authors' extensive experience in teaching and enabling learning
- Addresses some of the problems and constraints of engaging in reflection on practice to counter some of the uncritical claims made for reflection

www.openup.co.uk

OPEN UNIVERSITY PRESS
McGraw - Hill Education

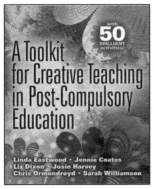

A TOOLKIT FOR CREATIVE TEACHING IN POST-COMPULSORY EDUCATION

Linda Eastwood, Jennie Coates, Liz Dixon, Josie Harvey, Chris Ormondroyd and Sarah Williamson

978-0-335-23416-5 (Paperback)
2009

eBook also available

This is the essential resource for trainees and teachers working in the PCET sector who are looking for new and creative ways of engaging and motivating their learners.

Key features:

- 50 practical and innovative teaching activities
- Variations and subject-specific examples
- Thinking Points to encourage reflection
- A theoretical framework which sets the activities within the context of creativity and innovation

www.openup.co.uk

OPEN UNIVERSITY PRESS
McGraw · Hill Education

CONTEMPORARY ISSUES IN LIFELONG LEARNING

Vicky Duckworth and Jonathan Tummons

9780335241125 (Paperback)
2010

eBook also available

This book provides an up-to-date and critical analysis of contemporary issues and debates in the lifelong learning sector (LLS). The authors examine significant issues in the LLS today including inclusive practice, the employability agenda, the curriculum in the LLS and research-led teaching.

There are practical strategies and reflective tasks that encourage readers to become critical, questioning practitioners. Other helpful features include:

- Learning outcomes at the beginning of each chapter
- Links to QTLS standards
- Case studies
- End of chapter summaries
- Further reading and useful websites

www.openup.co.uk